AF248925

PHILIP G. DUFFY

B to B MARKETING

CREATING & IMPLEMENTING A SUCCESSFUL BUSINESS TO BUSINESS MARKETING PROGRAM

PROBUS PUBLISHING COMPANY
Chicago, Illinois
Cambridge, England

ISBN 1-55738-299-9

Printed in the United States of America

BC

1   2   3   4   5   6   7   8   9   0

To Anne, Pat, Cathy and Mike

Table of Contents

Preface

This book addresses the needs of experienced practitioners who are seeking new solutions to traditional marketing challenges, as well as newer marketing analysts interested in drawing on others' experiences to improve their business-to-business marketing skills.

The topics covered are those most likely to surface routinely in the world of business marketing. Veteran practitioners typically seek ways to sharpen their skills; this is evidenced by the heavy attendance of experienced managers at business conferences and seminars. Often a lecture, an article, or a case study can stimulate the thinking process and help provide answers to vexing problems.

For the newer analysts, this volume serves as a training guide that addresses problems they can expect to encounter in the course of their careers. The true marketing professional, young or old, continually seeks new techniques and looks to benefit from the experience of more seasoned practitioners.

I view this not as a theoretical work, but rather as an effort to blend theory and practice into a single, easy-to-read volume. It offers solutions to the challenges marketing practitioners face virtually every day.

There are many good texts on marketing theory that are necessary for a basic understanding of the discipline. Conversely, many managers scoff at theory and rely heavily on their personal experiences. A blend of the two approaches—the academic and the real world—is necessary, and this volume is designed to meet that challenge.

This book also responds to the college-level need for practical material to supplement the theoretical approach taken by most textbooks. I have relied on this work as a text for my course in business-to-business marketing at Stonehill College in North Easton, Mass. The response has been overwhelmingly favorable from working practitioners looking to enhance their career skills, as well as full time students preparing to enter the field.

In a real sense, it is autobiographical, in that it represents a distillation of my forty years as an industrial marketing practitioner for major corporations and as a college instructor. My companies ranged from producers of heavy industrial products to sources of high-technology, computerized products.

I would like to thank writer/editor Dick Sherman for his editorial contributions during the preparation of the manuscript.

I also would like to acknowledge the encouragement, support, and assistance I received from my family as the work progressed toward its final form.

Philip G. Duffy
Sharon, MA

Introduction

This introduction provides:

- The definition of business-to-business marketing used in this book;
- The characteristics of business-to-business marketing; and
- Business-to-business marketing compared with consumer marketing.

Business-to-business marketing differs from its consumer counterpart in many important ways. Though many of the principles are the same, their execution may differ sharply. While engineering students must learn a broad spectrum of scientific disciplines, the practical application of those disciplines may be quite focused. The purpose of this volume is to provide guidelines to the application of business-to-business marketing principles. The following chapters will help the marketing practitioner avoid the potholes and detours that are altogether too common to the profession.

DEFINITION

Marketing encompasses the activities involved in getting goods from the producer to the consumer. For the purposes of this work, the business-to-business market comprises:

> Organizations that purchase products for their own use, for producing other products or for resale.

The customers are primarily commercial businesses, governments, and institutions. Therefore, this market includes large corporations as well as smaller companies that may manufacture or distribute limited products or services.

BUSINESS-TO-BUSINESS MARKETING CHARACTERISTICS

Marketing textbooks generally agree that certain differences exist between "consumer" and "business-to-business" marketing, although all do not identify the same differences. For the products under discussion here, the following characteristics are pertinent:

- Derived demand;
- Long negotiation periods;
- Relatively high value product;
- Requirements for after-sale service;
- Multiple buying influences;

♦ Geographic concentration;

♦ Fluctuating demand; and

♦ Inelastic demand.

Derived Demand

This term essentially postulates that the demand for industrial products is not created by the industrial user but by the user's customer. In other words, auto manufacturers do not buy machine tools for their satisfaction (as a consumer might buy a good book); they buy machine tools to satisfy the demand for automobiles that their customers generate. Therefore, in defining the market for industrial products, it is necessary to identify the industrial customers' ultimate market as well.

Long Negotiation Periods

Impulse drives many consumer products; that is, decision, negotiation, and purchase occur almost simultaneously. Even with larger purchases, such as homes or automobiles, quick decisions are common. However, with industrial purchases, the negotiating period may extend beyond a year. Such purchases must accommodate the following steps:

♦ Problem recognition;

♦ Definition of need;

♦ Product specifications;

♦ Supplier review;

♦ Proposal solicitation;

♦ Supplier selection;

♦ Purchase; and

♦ Post-purchase review.

Relatively High Value

Many industrial products are custom built and carry a high price tag. Even the more standard items are not produced in the volume of many consumer goods. Moreover, their quality may need to respond to precise application needs. Faulty products may cause a major manufacturing plant, utility, or refinery to close down, incurring tremendous costs. These conditions contribute to their traditionally higher value.

After-Sale Service

Because of the relative complexity of many industrial products and their high value, customers may require installation and start-up help. Further, these products may be used in processes that can be shut down only at great cost. Therefore, the availability of immediate help to deal with functional crises is essential. Many companies maintain regional service facilities to minimize potential time loss in responding to emergencies.

Multiple Buying Influences

Due to the generally higher cost and significance of these products, often the higher levels of management make the purchase decisions. Often the decision must be made or approved by the board of directors or a senior management committee. Hence, the vendor may be required to make presentations to several groups and sell his product or services to many individuals serving in various capacities. It can become a major problem to identify the real decision makers in these negotiations.

Geographic Concentration

Because of their sheer size, some manufacturers cannot pick up and move easily. Therefore, they tend to concentrate in areas that offer an adequate labor pool, good transportation, and other advantages. The concentration of the steel, automotive, and petroleum industries illustrates this point. A current example would be the concentration of the high-tech industries in the Silicon Valley in California and on the Route 128 belt outside Boston.

Fluctuating Demand

The demand on, and therefore the sales to, the industrial market fluctuate much more sharply than in the consumer sector. The peaks and valleys associated with the various phases of the business cycle are much more pronounced, making a chart of sales performance look like a series of icebergs. Part of this is due to the reaction of corporate managers to business conditions. Reductions in personnel and inventories often are delayed, awaiting the inevitable recovery. When that recovery appears elusive, restructuring is common. When the recovery does appear, there is a natural reluctance to engage in unbridled expansion. Painful memories are not easily shaken.

Inelastic Demand

Whereas the demand for consumer goods often relates to price levels, the demand for industrial goods is less price-sensitive. Even with price increases, customers who need the product will buy it to meet the demands of their customers. This does not imply that price is not important.

Price negotiations become tough as determined buyers attempt to get full value for their purchase. Their job performance depends on it.

BUSINESS-TO-BUSINESS AND CONSUMER MARKETING COMPARED

Often there is a distinction between industrial and consumer demand in the sense that the former is rational and the latter emotional. True, industrial buyers tend to analyze the product and the seller carefully, but so do many consumers, as evidenced by the popularity of such publications as *Consumer Reports.* The important consideration is that not *all* consumer buying is emotional, and not *all* industrial buying is purely rational. The personal relationships of trust and confidence often outweigh price and delivery as purchase determinants.

Although business-to-business marketing theoretically is not limited to major heavy or high-technology equipment, in this volume that will be the emphasis. In theory, items such as the pencils sold to consumers may be classed as industrial goods when sold to industrial customers. The reason: it is not the product that determines how it will be classed but rather how it is to be marketed. Pricing, advertising, packaging, and distribution will differ for products sold to an ultimate consumer rather than to an industrial customer. However, this volume concentrates on the industrial firm that produces or sells exclusively traditional industrial products.

In the chapters that follow, these characteristics and differences will be examined in discussions of marketing information systems, products, competition, distribution channels, sales forecasting, call reports, marketing planning, compensation, marketing costs, expense budgets, and the marketing audit. In each chapter, after the explanations of the theories, practical approaches, or "how-to" methods will be discussed.

Because the state of the art is changing rapidly in terms of computer hardware and software, solutions that were adequate a few years ago now may be outdated. Decisions on batch processing versus on-line, large computers versus desktop (or laptop), and selection of appropriate software are considerations that can change almost daily. Therefore, it behooves the individual practitioner to keep current with the technology. One must select the solutions available, realizing that changes will be required to keep up with the state of the art. The following pages share the practical experiences of many years in industry. Sometimes a quick fix must be applied to a panic situation. Sometimes managers with long experience fall back on their past successes and may not investigate alternatives. This is not a book of theory. It is a book dealing with daily problems and how many can be managed, if not solved completely. Read it as a guide, recognizing your situations and applying the general recommendations to your specific problems. Good luck!

1

Information Systems

Marketing information is a fundamental business tool. This chapter addresses the subject with the following major topics:

- Types of information systems often found in business-to-business marketing practice;

- The definition of a **marketing information system** as differentiated from other information systems;

- The justification for an information system;

- The necessity of building the system around user requirements;

- The challenges of system design with suggested considerations;

- Illustrations of viable information system output; and

- Problems often faced in the design and maintenance of marketing information systems.

How do you evaluate a practical business-to-business marketing program? This fundamental question faces all practitioners charged with running their organizations' marketing activities. Of the many points of entry, **information** is of primary concern, for without it, all other programs lack focus. There can be no question that information fuels any and all marketing endeavors. **Strategic audits,** internal and external, require their information early in the process. Availability is crucial. **Planning** and **forecasting** require a strong foundation of historical data. Both historical and current knowledge are essential to the planning process.

Competitive studies require detailed internal and external information. Without documentation, the data are general and unfocused.

Marketing cost and **call reporting** are related topics. Measuring their performance for improvement requires comparative internal and external information.

In order to develop a cogent analysis, such functions as budgets, distribution channels, sales compensation, and product analysis all require an understanding of the past plus a grasp of the relevant current circumstances. An information system is a key element.

Working from these concepts, information systems are presented in this first chapter. Discussion of these other important marketing activities proceeds from the general to the specific.

SYSTEM TYPES

Many of the system types listed in Figure 1-1 are related and, in fact, may evolve from a common database. This chapter concentrates on the marketing portion of this database and concerns itself with marketing input and processing.

DEFINITIONS

A marketing information system (MkIS), as defined by Pride and Ferrell in *Marketing: Basic Concepts and Strategies*, is:

> "...the framework for the day-to-day management and structuring of information gathered regularly from sources both inside and outside an organization."[1]

Figure 1-1 Types of Systems

Management Information Systems (MIS)

Marketing Information Systems (MkIS)

Executive Information Systems (EIS)

Executive Support Systems (ESS)

Decision Support Systems (DSS)

End-User Computing (EUC)

Expert Systems

Strategic Information Planning (SIP)

Individual companies may use slightly different definitions. The key point is that the system should involve a **continuing** effort, not merely a study for a specific project (like marketing research). The classic differentiation between marketing information systems and marketing research is that the former is a continuing process, and the latter a gathering of information for specific situations.

As part of this definition, data and information must be differentiated. Data is raw, unevaluated input. Information is evaluated data. Many people mistakenly use the terms interchangeably. This chapter concerns itself with **information** built upon **data.**

Sales versus Orders

The definition of the term "sales" also is important. This term may have different meanings depending upon the source. To sales and marketing people, sales mean new orders. To accounting and financial people, sales often refer to revenues, billings, or shipments, as in "net sales" on income statements. Using the term "new orders" in marketing information systems eliminates much confusion. Use the terms "shipments," "billings," or "revenues" when reporting the end-of-cycle activities.

Order Receipt Date

"When is an order an order?" is a question that requires definition. Companies have different answers for this question. The trite answer is: "When the president says it is an order." The more likely view states that an order is at least a verbal commitment from a customer of his intention to buy. More firmly, it refers to a bonafide purchase order or letter-of-intent from the customer, including provision for billing the customer if the order is cancelled. This term should be defined clearly, because significant time may elapse between a verbal commitment and receipt of a confirming purchase order. Further, the receipt date may affect financial records and credit for sales incentive.

NEED FOR INFORMATION

The justification of an MkIS is almost self-evident. Most marketing activities depend on information. The conversion of raw data is an information systems department (IS) function, an entirely separate activity with its own expertise. However, developing a system with useful output requires cooperation with marketing users.

The recognized need for information continues to grow. System developers have completed the transition of computer generated single use reports to computer databases that can be interrogated on demand for any combination of data elements. However, since intent here is to highlight that creation of an MkIS can be extremely complex, it is useful to examine the various remedies that can prevent major miscommunication, especially by users.

While current literature abounds with articles detailing sophisticated approaches to the generation of MkIS, not all companies are equipped to take advantage of the latest techniques. Some companies label their processes "strategic information systems." James Senn, addressing the subject in the Oct.-Dec. 1989 issue of *Business*, argues that it is the **use** of a system, **not its design** that makes it strategic.[2] Although the more sophisticated techniques are recognized, smaller organizations may be limited to less formal systems. These still require the emphasis to be on the **use.**

P. Sellers' March 13, 1989, article in *Fortune* states, ". . . the quality of any product or service is what the customer says it is."[3] The developer's opinion means little to the end user. This has been a problem for years because developers considered the job complete when the programs were written.

Since the marketers are the users, their involvement is of primary importance. Their needs (or the company budget), may not justify the cost of the state-of-the-art system. Many companies must proceed with minimum attention from the IS department.

USER REQUIREMENTS

An MkIS generates many uses for information. Some early system designers tried to identify them by discussing general needs with users. To their dismay, they found user needs often difficult to pre-determine; some users really do not know what they want until they see it. Others assume they will need only minimal information. Only after their systems are operational do they comprehend the need for more detailed information. Still other users want maximum information on a database, permitting retrieval of almost any kind of information. These varying needs require a meeting of the minds of the developers and users on the definition, content, and availability of the system.

Before attempting to design a marketing system, marketers should do their homework. A first step may involve a series of questions to probe specific needs. For example:

- What do we **want** to know?

- What do we **need** to know?

- **How often** do we need the information?

- **Who needs it** and who should get it?

- How **flexible** should it be?

- **Who has authority** to **change** the **system?**

- **Who has authority** to **change** the **data?**

- **Who is responsible** for **auditing** and **debugging?**

- How will **security** of data and output be handled?

- Who has **responsibility** for the system?

- Does it have **top management support?**

If the marketers and developers can answer these questions in advance, the first development meeting will be much more fruitful.

To answer these questions, marketers must identify their needs. Individual companies may add other categories, depending on their specific circumstances. More uses may surface later. The following is a typical list:

- Product planning and analysis;
- Industry planning and analysis;
- Competitive analysis;
- Current performance;
- Customer analysis;
- Market research;
- Retrofits or recalls;
- Forecasting; and
- Combinations of the above.

Product Planning and Analysis

For a company to review its current product lines and their performance, a consistent history must be developed. Using the computer as a high-speed adding machine provides listings of products and applications. However, a more detailed analysis is usually necessary to convert this data into information. Such analysis could resolve whether certain products appeared in combination with other products with some regularity. It may require identifying the customers, their location, price paid, application, etc. Analyses of this type broaden current and possibly future usage, leading to new product development.

Industry Planning and Analysis

Most products are sold across several industries. Other products traditionally are sold to specific industries in large quantities. Which industries are most important and perhaps most profitable? If a supplier is gaining or losing position in an identifiable industry, a power shift in the market may be responsible. Further, a supplier organized along industry lines needs information on the regular performance and penetration of its customers.

The array of products currently sold to the nuclear power industry highlights the need. Before the nuclear accident occurred at Three Mile

Island in Pennsylvania, certain companies had dedicated entire product groups to the nuclear power industry. Others sold both to the nuclear and conventional power industries. Without the ability to establish the amount of anticipated nuclear business, a supplier would be unable to plan its future. While the need for power still exists, it has shifted from the nuclear sector toward other sources of energy.

Competitive Analysis

A stated purpose of strategic information systems is competitive analysis. This type of information once was gathered quietly. Today it is highly publicized. The sporting world is an excellent example of the importance of this tool. Athletic teams routinely scout their opponents. Building a database containing competitors' performances provides instant access to likely competitive scenarios. A profile of each competitor provides a history and current business performance. Extrapolated to the likely competitive response to new products, price changes, or current negotiations, this information represents a powerful tool.

Current Performance

Marketing departments regularly require information on their own present and past performances. Other departments, such as sales, finance, economics, manufacturing, and general management also might require this information. Examples of required performance information include:

- Orders from a particular industry in a specific area;
- The product volume sold to an individual customer;
- A list of customers who placed orders for specific products;
- Discounts by product or type of customer; and
- Volume of business through each distribution outlet.

Sales incentive programs require current performance information for credit assignment and quota comparisons. The information system is the official "scorekeeper" of orders entered and their revisions.

Financial considerations differ from marketing requirements. If reports are on a financial basis, a continual series of order adjustments must be made, with the adjustments occurring in the current month. For example, an order booked in January and cancelled in March shows the cancellation (negative booking) in March. The original order still appears in the January log. However, an economics department might want to know the date of the original order. Here the cancellation in a particular month is somewhat artificial, and economists may want to consider the booking as never having occurred.

Marketing people, on the other hand, prefer to work in the current period. For example, consider an order booked in December and cancelled the following March. Marketing would not want to absorb the cancellation penalty in March, since the order occurred in a prior year. This is particularly important where current year operations determine sales incentive payments. Marketing base performance measurement has advantages. However, some orders will be duplicated if each year is handled separately. All users must have access to information suitable for their specific needs. This may require the ability to run output reports in several formats.

Order status is another application of present performance. Given this data, salespeople can keep customers informed of scheduled shipments without checking with the home office.

Aged backlog reports show months of scheduled shipment for everything booked and not yet shipped. Typically, loads for the near-term months are heaviest, with less scheduled in the future months. This information is critical for manufacturing planning and for forecasting.

Customer Analysis

It is no longer enough to know that a supplier company booked millions of dollars from many customers. Also critical is the volume associated with each customer, his buying patterns, and in which facility his orders originate. Relationships with other suppliers identify the real value of a customer. A company contemplating extending quantity or blanket discounts to large users must be armed with an accurate profile of the customer. Without it, the program is likely to fail.

Market Research

Historical information must be available to conduct any realistic market research. As a continuous process, an information system provides this information in reports or retrievals. This allows flexibility in the design of the research project and the analysis of results. These results may show little change in the product performance or industry performance just from a new approach to the market. On the other hand, favorable, though opposite, results may occur. Past, present, and projected information are essential to the validity of the market research.

Retrofits or Recalls

Most readers will recognize the term "retrofits" in the context of the auto industry, where they are described as recalls. A retrofit calls for the notification of all purchasers for correction of a certain defect. Not merely a convenience, recalls can prevent serious accidents and lawsuits.

Forecasting

Sound forecasting (a topic covered in detail in Chapter 5), requires a history of the company, product, industry, and whatever other variable may be at issue. A forecast must evolve from reference points that cover both past and present. A marketing information system can be used to gather history and make projections. Data search and computation can be tedious and at times misleading unless consistency and validity are built into the process.

Combination Analysis

The above categories have dealt with such considerations as product, industry, and customer. All these factors are necessary for some analyses. Often a user requests information and is certain of the need. Yet, when results are available, it is not uncommon for users to report changed needs, perhaps becoming more detailed. Ideally, the system can extract anything on the database or history file in any combination, despite the fact that such combinations never were foreseen. These conditions require computerization because of:

- ◆ The sheer volume of data;

- ◆ The need for consistent and accurate processing; and

- ◆ The various combinations of data handled.

SYSTEM DESIGN

Designing and running MkIS present special challenges. Before examining them, the following provides a brief procedure. Several textbooks cover this process, which is not unlike the procedures associated with any new product development. Richard Cardinale, Chairman, MIS at Central Connecticut University, suggests the following elements might be found in most cycles:[4]

- ◆ Project definition;

- ◆ Feasibility study;

- ◆ Project development and design;

- ◆ Acceptance testing;

- ◆ Installation/implementation; and

- ◆ Post-implementation maintenance.

These steps in the process require some explanation.

Project Definition

This important step defines the problem to be solved. Project definition meetings should include senior management, users, and the developers. As in any new product blueprint, the scope and purpose must be defined.

From this charter comes the formation of project teams and the assignment of an overall project manager. Both are significant, since the former represent the user communities, and the latter must guide a diverse group of participants.

Expectations must be detailed, budgets determined, and assignments and schedules targeted. It should be recognized that the purpose is to create a new operating system, not merely to mechanize a manual system. Since there are representatives from several disciplines, it is important to create a set of workable definitions. Experience shows these will be used constantly.

Feasibility Study

Users often nurture unrealistic expectations; moreover, the capabilities of the IS (Information Systems) personnel or equipment may be limiting factors. With problem definition complete, it may be necessary to use trade-offs between desires and abilities. Cost and time constraints must be considered as well. It is important that users recognize the need for their continued participation. Feasibility discussions should confirm this.

Project Development and Design

Through this is usually the province of the MkIS developers, users must participate fully as well. Users should understand the concept steps and involve themselves in the value of subsystems as work progresses. The **project** is only as precise as the original current knowledge, whereas the **process** is an evolving one.

Users should contribute in the review of questions such as:

♦ **Centralized versus decentralized system:** Though centralized may be more desirable from a processing point of view, decentralized may be much better from a field input perspective.

♦ **On-line versus batch retrieval:** Overnight access often is sufficient. However, immediate access may be equally critical.

♦ **The form of output:** Specific hard-copy reports are valuable. Because different users have different needs, the ability to create new formats while accessing the data may be preferable.

Acceptance Testing

This step gives IS personnel the ability to evaluate their work. While complex programming or data handling requires confirmation of procedures, this alone is not enough; a successful technology does not necessarily mean a satisfied user. If preliminary output does not provide the expected satisfaction, the process is not yet a success. Now team members can really look at their tests in light of their blueprints. It would not be unusual if the rules of the game had changed slightly in the process due to changes in personnel, organization, equipment, or some other variable.

Installation and Implementation

Once the acceptance test has satisfied management, users, and developers, it is ready to be implemented. The question is whether the process should go on stream piecemeal or at one time. If it is replacing another system, they should run in parallel temporarily so as to retain existing operations. Also, an evolutionary start can serve as an additional live test. Here again, the users are integral to the process.

Post-Implementation Maintenance

IS people can never declare a system complete and walk away from it. The need for improvements and changes requires the ongoing expertise of IS people to maintain the system. Moreover, users often develop new requests that challenge the developers.

Data to Be Captured

An obvious question involves **the data to be captured** to provide sufficient information. Consider the following useful items:

- Product (subdivided as necessary);

- Industry (also subdivided as necessary);

- Customer name and address;

- Location (buyer versus user versus influencer);

- Salespersons responsible for order;

- Application;

- Currency (important for international); and

- Price (list, net, and discount by individual product).

TYPES OF OUTPUT

Even with the current tendency to provide on-line access to databases, there is always a need for standardized reports on a regular basis. It may be desirable to limit access to the database for security reasons. After all, these files contain sensitive information that is not for all eyes.

Generally, necessary information includes at a minimum product, industry, value, and location. Figure 1-2 portrays a table referencing individual product orders by branch office. This could be by country rather than domestic branch for those companies engaged in international business. (Note that branch totals are included in the last column to the right and product totals listed at the bottom of the page.)

Figure 1-3 displays industry orders by branch office. The industries are totaled at the bottom of the page. Industry orders by product line are shown in Figure 1-4. This matrix provides valuable summary information.

Figure 1-2

PRODUCT ORDERS BY BRANCH
JAN-OCT 1990
in $1,000

BRANCH	MTRS	PUMPS	PULLEY	CONTR	BOILER	OVEN	CHAIN	BRANCH TOTAL
Boston								
New York								
Philadelphia								
Wilmington								
Washington								
Pittsburgh								
Cleveland								
Cincinnati								
Detroit								
Chicago								
Kansas City								
Tulsa								
Houston								
Denver								
Seattle								
San Francisco								
Los Angeles								
PRODUCT TOTAL								

Figure 1-3

INDUSTRY ORDERS BY BRANCH
JAN-OCT 1990
in $1,000

BRANCH OFFICE	UTIL	PETR	CHEM	FOOD	PAPER	METALS	BRANCH TOTAL
Boston							
New York							
Philadelphia							
Wilmington							
Washington							
Pittsburgh							
Cleveland							
Cincinnati							
Detroit							
Chicago							
Kansas City							
Tulsa							
Houston							
Denver							
Seattle							
San Francisco							
Los Angeles							

INDUSTRY TOTAL

Figure 1-4

INDUSTRY ORDERS BY PRODUCT
JAN-OCT 1990
in $1,000

PRODUCT	UTIL	PETR	CHEM	FOOD	PAPER	METALS	PRODUCT TOTAL
ELECTRIC MOTORS							
Foot Mounted							
Flanged							
PUMPS							
PULLEYS							
CHAIN & BELTS							
CONTROLS							
Electronic							
Pneumatic							
BOILERS							
Commercial							
Marine							
OVENS							
INDUSTRY TOTAL							

The handling of revisions often raises questions on format. Figure 1-5 illustrates one approach to this problem. The list of branches is self-explanatory. The top listing definitions are as follows:

- Column 1: Backlog (orders booked but not yet shipped) as of the first of the year;

- Column 2: Orders booked year-to-date, including revisions (upward or downward) to these orders;

- Column 3: Revisions only to prior year's orders;

- Column 4: Shipments, year-to-date; and

- Column 5: Backlog, year-to-date, at month's end. This backlog is the algebraic sum of the first four columns. This helpful total tells whether orders are exceeding shipments or vice-versa.

Figure 1-6 is similar to Figure 1-5 except it reports product information. The benefits are similar. Many other combinations can be produced from data in the computer files. Besides current year operations, other combinations may be essential, including history by product, industry, customer, and/or geography. Customer planning programs, discount policies, and the like demand this information. Obviously, the combinations are legion.

PROBLEMS

No treatise on information systems would be complete without identifying possible problems. While building teams, specifications, and sequence, these potential roadblocks must be considered:

Lack of Management Interest

Implementation and continuation of a marketing information system can be very expensive. Management should recognize at the outset the need for major commitments in terms of time, money, and personnel. Support from the top is essential. This interest and support must be obvious to the entire organization. If management sets the tone, the other echelons will respond accordingly.

Figure 1-5

TOTAL ORDERS BY BRANCH
JAN-OCT 1990
in $1,000

BRANCH OFFICE	JAN 1 BACKLOG	YR-TO-DATE ORDERS	PRIOR YR REVISIONS	YR-TO-DATE SHIPMENTS	OCT 31 BACKLOG
Boston					
New York					
Philadelphia					
Wilmington					
Washington					
Pittsburgh					
Cleveland					
Cincinnati					
Detroit					
Chicago					
Kansas City					
Tulsa					
Houston					
Denver					
Seattle					
San Francisco					
Los Angeles					
Y–T–D TOTALS					

Figure 1-6

TOTAL ORDERS BY PRODUCT
JAN-OCT 1990
in $1,000

PRODUCT	JAN 1 BACKLOG	YR-TO-DATE ORDERS	PRIOR YR REVISIONS	YR-TO-DATE SHIPMENTS	OCT 31 BACKLOG
ELECTRIC MOTORS					
Foot Mounted					
Flanged					
PUMPS					
PULLEYS					
CHAIN & BELTS					
CONTROLS					
Electronic					
Pneumatic					
BOILERS					
Commercial					
Marine					
OVENS					
Y–T–D TOTALS					

Lack of Timely Input

Most champions of marketing information systems consider timeliness vitally important. A major benefit is availability of timely information for decision-making. Most companies today are making strong efforts to get prompt, if not real-time, information. If various segments submit data "when they can," a basic pillar of effectiveness will be lost. Here again, management's support is crucial.

Lack of Support by Information Systems Department

In a large company, IS creates the technical portion of a computer-based system. If IS fails to provide qualified personnel for systems analysis, programming, and debugging, development will drag and may never come to fruition. If IS personnel are not available for maintenance, inaccuracies may occur and timeliness may be destroyed. Smaller systems using only stand-alone personal computers may not experience this dependency.

Inattention to Input

In smaller systems without electronic input, individuals may be charged with supplying manual input. Any input prepared carelessly results in output of little value. Some examples of inattention include: inaccurate product or customer coding; careless handling of prices and discounts; improper identification of salespeople or industry; and lack of end user identification. Even if an audit program carefully scans the input and output, valuable time may be lost or extra costs incurred.

Codes and Coding

Marketing systems often have elaborate codes to allow for easy handling in a computer. **Industry codes** normally are based on the Standard Industrial Classification code (SIC), published by the Office of Management and Budget (OMB) of the U.S. government.[5] In a multinational corporation, the basis for industry codes may be the International Standard Industrial Classification (ISIC), published by the United Nations.[6] In either case, all participants in the system must use the same codes.

   Customer codes allow ready identification of the buyer and user. These may be two different organizations. Once established, a customer code may provide cross-references to salesperson, industry, country, and branch office. This makes it unnecessary to identify the salesperson or industry for every order. It therefore minimizes judgment errors.

Control of coding is basic but time-consuming. The question of centralized versus decentralized assignment must be answered. If the latter, duplication must be prevented. Since many people use the codes, the availability of a current listing is critical.

Dealing in **different currencies** requires a currency conversion to U.S. dollars. The official conversion rate may change daily. Accounting departments often set policies on this matter. For monthly financial reports, they may settle on a month-end value. For current information, daily or weekly averages may be used. The *Wall Street Journal* reports this information daily.

Product codes may contain more than ten digits, including dashes and other characters. Computerized systems are not very forgiving if these designations are handled carelessly. Faulty product codes may cause rejection or shipment of improper products.

Lack of Total Company Coordination

A manager or coordinator is necessary to control all codes, input, output, documentation, and policies. This individual serves as an interface between IS and users. If several people attempt to change codes, programs, or policies without control, chaos results. The marketing group probably is the best source of this coordinator.

Inadequate Information

It is impossible to anticipate all types of information users may later require. Nonetheless, some likely combinations are obvious. If the system captures price data, it also should record discounts. Customer information should include credit and tax data and zip codes for billing addresses. Product information must be specific for manufacturing and should provide for retrofits.

Errors

Cross checks in the programming can eliminate many errors. Even with perfect logic in the programs, faulty input data will cause faulty output. Programs cannot always recognize incorrect numerical data. Experienced persons should scan output for reasonable values and discrepancies.

Other Problems

Little things can be bothersome. For example, use of the letter "O" instead of the numeral zero "0" can create problems. Power failures happen. The simple decimal point can create havoc. Untrained personnel can slow the process. In practice, the unexpected and obvious can cause many delays and frustrations.

SUMMARY

The marketing information system is a **fundamental business tool.** All other marketing activities depend on information in some way. The question is not whether to have a system, but how complex it should be. Smaller organizations may find a personal-computer-based system more than adequate. Very large corporations may require on-line processes as decision support systems.

Designing the system requires more than handling of data to produce reports. It requires qualitative input as well, best supplied by the users. Since these users may not always appreciate the appearance of the output, they must be involved throughout the process. Senior management also must participate in the development. Their use of the final information and their stamp of approval are factors that will influence the attention given to the development.

This chapter provides suggested formats. However, the type of output is a function of the company and its specific needs. Each firm must determine its requirements.

In any case, certain procedures must be followed and certain questions answered. Inherent problems will be similar, whatever the size of the company. The complexity of the system will vary with the specific needs of the time.

Using the above guidelines, define the system carefully. Identify the support of management and users, and emphasize understanding to keep them communicating with the developers. Monitor the output, and update the system as needs change. Recognize that a system can never remain static but is in a constant state of creative evolution.

REFERENCES

1. Pride, William M., and Ferrell, O.C., *Marketing: Basic Concepts and Strategies*, 7th ed., Boston, MA: Houghton Mifflin Co., 1989, p. 198. Original source was Andrea Dunham, "Information Systems Are the Key to Managing Future Business Needs," from *Marketing News*, May 23, 1986, p. 11.
2. Senn, James A., "Information Systems Strategies," *Business*, Oct.-Dec. 1989, pp. 43-47.
3. Sellers, P., "Getting Customers to Love You," *Fortune*, March 13, 1989, p. 39.
4. Cardinale, Richard, "User Involvement—An Assessment of the Need for This Vital Link in the System Development Process," *Information Executive*, Fall 1990, p. 39.
5. United States Office of Management and Budget, *Standard Industrial Classification Manual*, Washington, D.C., 1987.
6. See *The International Standard Industrial Classification* and the *U.S. Standard Industrial Classification*. Technical Paper No. 14, U.S. Department of Commerce.

2

Products

Business-to-business marketing activities center on the product line. All attention focuses on how to bring the product to the customer.

To assist in understanding this process, the following product factors are presented.

- The definition of an industrial product;

- Definition and characteristics of the industrial market;

- The importance of supporting and maintaining present products; and

- New product development, with a suggested action plan, and consideration of problem areas and success rates.

What is an industrial product? Is it industrial because it is used in industry? If so, many products that can be used in either the consumer or industrial markets are industrial products (for example, a personal computer).

Further, what does "industry" mean? Is the term limited to customers who manufacture items? For our purposes here, industrial products are physical items or services sold by manufacturers or their distribution channels to business firms. The latter include other manufacturers, channel members, schools, hospitals, and governments: in short, all customers except ultimate consumers who buy for their own satisfaction. These products dictate a type of marketing approach that differs greatly from retailing.

THE PRODUCT

Definitions abound regarding the discrete grouping of products. Some classify products based on whether the purchase is an expense or capital item, whether it becomes part of the final product, or whether the product is a stock item or built to specifications, to name a few. Some definitions treat services separately, while in many companies, services become an integral adjunct to the product. Our emphasis here is on machinery, equipment, and materials, which usually experience similar problems in distribution, expenses, forecasting, and the like. Essentially, then, the discussions and examples involve capital goods. Other products may well use the same techniques to solve their difficulties. Marketing problems are not unique to capital good products. The term "product" will be used in this context, and will include physical goods or their related services.

THE MARKET

There are far fewer industrial customers than there are retail customers. To understand the categories of industry, the broadest classifications are listed in Figure 2-1.[1]

It is useful to classify markets this way, since many reporting systems do so, and good comparative information is thus readily available. For example, the U.S. Department of Commerce uses this classification in many of its statistical tables. Also, other companies that publicly forecast capital expenditures of industry use these same groupings. This approach

Figure 2-1

MANUFACTURING

Durable Goods

    Primary metals

    Fabricated metals

    Electrical machinery

    Machinery except electrical

    Transportation equipment

    Stone, clay, and glass

    Other durables

Nondurable Goods

    Food and beverage

    Textiles

    Paper

    Chemicals

    Petroleum

    Rubber

    Other nondurables

NONMANUFACTURING

Public Utilities

    Electric

    Gas and other

Transportation

    Railroad

    Air

    Other

Mining

Commercial and Other

    Wholesale and retail

    Finance and insurance

    Personal and business

        services

    Communications

is helpful in classifying one's own business, and in reviewing customer industries for insights into their historical patterns, relative movements, and present and predicted performances. The need for breadth in the definition of industry is evident.

These industries broadly define the marketplace. Most of them can be, or should be, prospects for orders. Companies must define their targets. This may depend on past market penetration or planned entry. One tenet of business-to-business marketing is the small number of buyers, and even the broad classes listed in Figure 2-1 result in a minimal number of actual accounts.

THE ORGANIZATION

Having defined the product and the marketplace, the third leg of this tripod is the organization. It is safe to say there exists no classic product marketing organization. Firms vary in this matter by size, product, and philosophy. Change is not uncommon. As companies reorganize or restructure, the product marketing operation often changes as well.

Product Managers

It is equally difficult to define the term "product manager," as used in industry. Some firms consider the product specialists in the staff marketing division as product managers, even though they bear no responsibility for price or profit. Other firms give the product manager full responsibility for selling, pricing, order entry, customer service, and profit. In the latter, if the line is not profitable, the product manager's responsibility is to adjust the marketing mix to make it profitable, to revise the line, or to discontinue it. There are many variations between these two extremes. The following chapters examine these marketing functions. For ease of discussion, the "accountable product manager" definition will be used. The functional performance, more than the title of the manager, is most important.

The product manager essentially runs a current business within the firm. One of his or her jobs is to ensure product completeness. This does not mean maintaining every size of every product. Some companies concentrate on large products or special applications. To know the line is to know the market, and what sizes or types the customers need. There should be no obvious gaps in the line and no unnecessary overlaps. Products do become obsolete. Customer needs or competitive offerings put a price on keeping up with change.

Technology changes rapidly, even in products once thought to be solid and unvarying. The product manager's responsibility is to lead, or at least keep up, in the technology race. New materials, new controls, and better quality, all contribute to a superior and more competitive product. Keeping pace in this area requires constant interface with the engineering and manufacturing functions, and their influences and contributions.

What kind of person is the typical product manager? Of primary value is a sales or marketing background. The differentiation lies between **sales,** the group dealing directly with customers, and **marketing,** the typical advisory group working in staff positions. Of critical concern is the need for an appreciation of customer problems, real or perceived. Unfortunately, not everyone shares an adequate level of sensitivity concerning customer feelings and perceptions. Some company people consider customer concerns interruptions to the flow of daily business. In the realm of capital goods, a technical background is also important. The ability to relate, to listen, and to learn is essential, if for no other reason than to develop relationships with the accounting, manufacturing, and engineering functions.

The product manager also requires a strong support organization to help carry out regular assignments. Ideally these team members would share similar characteristics, but many may be more junior, suitable candidates for later promotion. Also, there is need for backup when the manager is absent. Staff reductions must not penalize this first line operation.

Product Positioning

Part of the product knowledge involves positioning the product in the marketplace. Some companies, known as high-cost, quality producers, may try to enter the low-price end of a product line by offering a lesser version. When years of promotion have created the quality position, the cheap version contradicts a carefully nurtured image. Also, positioning the product vis-a-vis the competition, whether by price or performance, is a necessary activity.

Selling "hardware only" was once the goal of many firms. When the supplier sells a "system," the customer has a right to expect a certain level of performance. The producer essentially is selling a solution to a problem rather than merely hardware. Solution selling requires much more of a sales organization and requires a product designed for the unified approach. This imposes greater responsibility and accountability for performance on the product marketing department. Differentiation from competition is often the approach used by systems sellers.

Product Pricing

In some companies, product pricing is a staff function outside of sales. The intent is to have a neutral group, without vested interests, responsible for consistent price policy for all products. However, where a product manager is responsible for profit, that manager also wants to control price. If the price is too low, it may generate many orders but result in little or no profit. If the price is too high, the demand may dry up. In either case, the responsibility lies with the product manager, and his job may be at stake. This obviously requires a knowledge of cost. Knowing the cost is high is not sufficient. It may take a cooperative effort with others in the company to reduce the cost to competitive levels.

Competitive Products

Product managers should be armed with competitive knowledge. Since the product manager is to a certain extent a product specialist, he should know the competitors, their products, and their likely strategies under varying conditions. Chapter 3 treats this topic in detail. This information is necessary for selecting the product sizes and types, and for pricing.

PRODUCT LIFE CYCLE

Every product has a life cycle. In consumer products, that life cycle may be measured in weeks, whereas an industrial installation may have a life of 30 years. The four phases of the traditional life cycle are listed below.

- ◆ Introduction;

- ◆ Growth;

- ◆ Maturity; and

- ◆ Decline.

Aberrations to this cycle are discussed later in the chapter. Figure 2-2 displays the traditional life cycle.[2] If a company knows where it truly stands in terms of the product life cycle, it can initiate certain actions, especially if the product is nearing the end of its useful life. An explanation of the life cycle phases follows:

1. **The first phase is the introduction.** Here, a new product enters the marketplace, and every effort is devoted to persuading customers that it is superior to prior offerings. The early sellers of personal computers successfully convinced customers that this new technology was faster and more accurate than their manual

Figure 2-2 The Four Stages of the Product Life Cycle

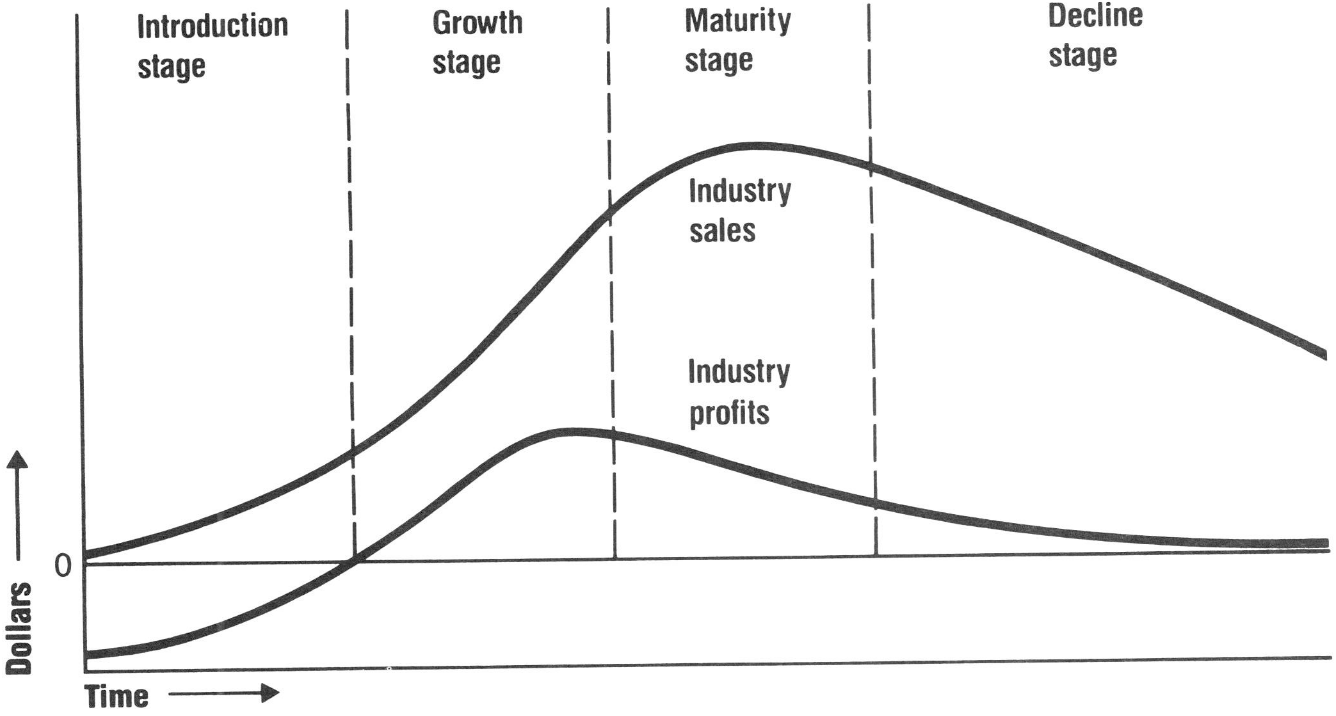

operations. The product growth rate is slow at the start, but begins to accelerate as customers begin to buy and benefit from the product's value.

2. **The second phase is the growth stage.** Here, sales begin to rise rapidly as customers accept the product and use it as a substitute for existing products. During this phase, it is usual for competitors to enter the market with similar products. This foments even greater growth to the entire market but takes its toll on the profit of the original manufacturer. The added competition drives down prices. The entry and proliferation of clones of the original personal computers exemplify this stage.

3. **The third phase is the maturity stage.** With acceptance, the product gains popularity and may continue at the top of the curve for some time. If there is nothing superior to replace it, and it is a necessary or desirable product, this phase may last for a long time. The acceptance of the desk-top computer is an example.

4. **The final stage in the cycle is decline.** This may occur when new products replace the original or when changes in technology obsolete the original. Another factor could be the inability of suppliers to retain quality at new, higher levels. Here, the decline continues until the company finally discontinues the product. The slide rule, so long a staple in mathematical circles, has encountered this fate.

Other Cycles

As pointed out, this is the traditional view of the product life cycle. However, in addition to this typical "S-shaped" curve, it is possible to have a recycle—that is, a decline followed by another brief growth and mature phase before final decline. Another shape involves the scalloped curve, where several humps develop as new uses develop for the product or new promotional campaigns give it a boost. Therefore, it is best not to assume that the first slowing of growth is going to lead to a decline. Reviews should be instituted to see whether these are false, short declines on the path to a far higher, final peak.

All products need not disappear after they have passed through the maturity phase. Companies continually look for ways to rejuvenate their older product lines. The consumer field often finds new uses for certain products, giving them a new lease on life. Industrial products also may be rejuvenated by expanding distribution channels, cutting prices to a level that will build volume and retain profits, or by using such products in new applications or industries.

THE PRESENT PRODUCT LINE

All product lines must be subjected to a regular surveillance program. A one-time star product may now decline to the maintenance level due to technology changes, competitive offerings, or changed market needs. These developments need not come as unpleasant surprises. Good product planning (discussed in Chapter 7) examines present situations of sales, performance, competition, and planned activity. Any major changes in the product and its future should surface here. Market planning examines individual order trends, industry penetration, and profitability. In some companies, specific groups conduct regular reviews of current products. Even an informal product review committee can ensure that product erosion does not go unnoticed.

Some current products may enjoy extended life cycles, whereby their configuration and performance may change little over time. Such products nonetheless require careful ongoing attention, whether technically or in terms of customer acceptance. Without being encouraged by regular promotion by sales and advertising, the customer base may erode from lack of focus. This daily maintenance of market activity sometimes overshadows the need to examine the product line for expansion or pruning.

Market Share

Many companies concentrate on market share studies to alert them to the need for remedial action. Clearly, knowing relative market share is important. For some products, this information is readily available from trade association statistics. Usually these are more timely than census figures and represent order levels rather than shipments. Monthly federal government statistics also provide good data. The practitioner must study the content of these sources for their validity with regard to his product. A workable solution is to create a marketing council within the trade association, its assignment being to define the categories required and encourage member participation. Such a statistical program can establish changes in the volume, if not always the absolute industry totals. There always will be some who will not report.

New Life for Older Products

If a product line is declining, it may respond to enhancements. Better performance, improved appearance, lower pricing, and more promotion all might serve to restore higher sales levels. Selective pruning of less popular sizes or less profitable configurations often rejuvenates the line. This is not as drastic as discarding the line or selling it off, either of which may have negative effects on employees, especially sales people. To estimate the importance of retaining a line, one might ask whether the firm would develop the line if it did not already have it.

Post-Sale Servicing of Customers

Post-sale service is an important corollary to any product. In the industrial field, placing the order does not end the sale. Order placement is only one step in the continuing relationship between buyer and seller. To win the order, the salesperson may have worked for months, even years, to establish trust with the customer. That customer does not expect this relationship to cease upon order placement. It is an ongoing process that includes advice on applications, shipment schedules, etc.

Product Service

An additional area of customer expectation involves product service. Many industrial products are so complex that they include installation services with the order. Even if not included in the price, customers often request supervision of installation or at least training sessions for the equipment operators. Also, some industrial products control customer processes that should not be shut down. This calls for the availability of prompt service and parts from the producer. Customers rely on this service; it goes with the product. Any decline in supplier responsiveness may take that supplier off the list of favored sources.

NEW PRODUCT DEVELOPMENT

There is always much interest in new products. They imply progress and challenge, a move into new areas. However, this can be a mixed blessing.

There are times when firms take on new products, either designed internally or purchased from an inventor or smaller company, where there is no fit within the company for that product. When enthusiasm runs high, company personnel may ignore the logical analysis that should precede adoption. The result is heavy spending on fruitless endeavors.

Sources of New Product Ideas

Ideas for new products come from many sources: customers with specific needs, company employees, marketplace demands, flankers to competitive products that are proving successful, inventors, stockholders, and almost any other source connected in any way with the company. Unless the company has a policy on new products and procedures on how to handle them, there may be so many ideas that they overwhelm the responsible departments.

Development Process

To forestall such situations, many companies adopt a new product screening process. Some use as few as two steps (concept identification and commercialization), others use a somewhat standardized ten-step process, while still others adopt something between these extremes. It is important to adopt a standard process, although steps may be skipped for some introductions. See Figure 2-3 for the steps often prescribed.[3] The terminology may differ among practitioners, but the steps are essentially the same.

The degree of complexity of these steps varies by company. It is possible to be quite sophisticated in approach. Other firms will skip the mathematical relationships and carry out the process qualitatively and simply.

The approach here is simple but tested, and contains the necessary ingredients for new product screening. The process is not really a set of individual steps but, rather, is evolutionary in nature. Activity among the various functions calls for a continuing interface to share ideas, resolve problems, and create solutions.

If the new product is an enhancement or is to flank an existing product, risk is minimal. However, if the concept is for a new-to-the-industry product, risk is heightened. Some managers shy away from too much risk because the stakes are high, in both funds and reputation. But there is also a risk in not developing new products—the risk of missing good market opportunities. This calls for good management judgment.

Figure 2-3

NEW PRODUCT DEVELOPMENT

TEN-STEP PROCESS

- Opportunity: a resource or a problem;

- Concept: an idea, plus a clear benefit statement;

- Tested Concept: customer screened and need is confirmed;

- Protocol: statement of benefits and features;

- Prototype: a tentative physical product;

- Specifications: exactly what the product is to be;

- Pilot: the product produced in the first process;

- Production: product produced in scale-up process;

- Market: product actually marketed, market test/launch; and

- Success: Product meets the goals set, profit.

NEW PRODUCT ORGANIZATION

A new products process requires a new products manager. Smaller companies do not need to make this a full-time position. However, larger companies with continual flows of new products should have specific positions. This takes a unique individual, a person who can direct a team without line authority over that team. The manager must have strong product management skills and be a creative problem-solver. He or she will direct a team—either functional people on loan, an assigned permanent staff, or a separate venture group. Since these people come from different disciplines, strong personal skills are important.

The manager should report to the company president. Reporting that high in the company gives the stamp of approval to the position and gives the new product manager access to the top management. Where new products are viable tools in expansion plans, the firm also should have a new products committee to oversee all new products. This committee might be composed of four or five members of senior management from different functions and should include the new products manager. All new products initially would be approved by this committee, which would follow the progress of any product in the stream.

PLAN OF ACTION

To provide for consistency in the development of new products over a period of time, the following will help:

Prepare Overall Documentation Manual

A written program provides the consistency necessary for continual operation. This is more than a check-off list; it is an approved program, easily understood by all in the company. The following pages present an example of a documented program. Different companies will use different categories, but this example can serve as a blueprint upon which to base the design of your program. With this documentation, many foolish and time-wasting suggestions surface along with good concepts. However, the former are easy to identify and discard. The introduction should cover company objectives as enumerated in the company management guide or mission statement. Clear statements should reference product areas or industries that are of prime interest; the influence of present distribution channels, and corporate price and profit philosophy also should be considered.

Preliminary Screening

A preliminary screening form supplies the basis for further evaluation. It should identify the person submitting the idea and should be dated. The form goes to the product committee, which decides whether the idea has enough merit to proceed. This process allows consideration by representatives of several disciplines, and is not just a marketing or engineering decision. Figure 2-4 illustrates a suggested format. Do not expect the idea originator to have detailed answers to all the suggested topics. These topics highlight the factors important to the initial product evaluation. They may cause the originator to search deeper into the desirability of the product or even abandon the idea because of market size, distribution needs, or capital requirements.

Figure 2-4

NEW PRODUCTS CHECKLIST

Submitted by:_____________________________   Date:_______________

1. Product description (include objectives):

2. Commercial aspects:

      a. Identify prospective industries:

      b. Identify types of customers:

      c. Identify known competitors:

      d. Estimated market size (dollars and/or units):

      e. Market requirements (price, service, reputation, etc.):

      f. Identify uses and applications:

3. Do patents or royalties exist on this product?

4. Facility requirements:

      a. What will manufacturing require?

      b. How much capital is needed?

      c. Estimate number and type of additional personnel.

5. What is the long-term profit outlook?

Identify the Chief Functions

The suggested process assumes that the chief functions in the company
are marketing (including sales, distribution, and advertising), engineering
(including R&D), manufacturing, and administration (accounting, legal,
information systems, etc.). The following discussion, pictured on the flow
chart in Figure 2-5, follows this organization. Readers should substitute
their own organizational formats.

Flow Chart Steps

Phase One: The screening form submitted to the product committee trig-
gers a preliminary investigation if the committee sees the concept as suitable. This study does not involve great expense; it is, as the name implies,
preliminary. The proposal would be presented to marketing and engineering, shown in the chart as Phase 1, to get impressions based on a cursory
review. If the consensus is negative, the project would be rejected. If positive, an intermediate study, Phase 2, would commence.

Phase Two: The various functional organizations would conduct more
detailed studies.

- Marketing would forecast orders, estimate market needs, and distribution requirements;

- Engineering would create preliminary designs and estimate pattern
  and tooling needs;

- Manufacturing would estimate machinery and equipment needs
  and look for material problems; and

- Administration would check legal questions regarding patents and
  trademarks, costs, profits, and personnel needs.

Expenses begin to mount during this final screening. These activities
are not routine. Forecasting alone is a difficult task. With an entirely new
product, there is little basis for comparison. Here, judgment and a willing-
ness to share concepts in confidence with good customers often yield the
best results. When the results continue to be positive, recommendations
go to the company president for his approval. Now the chief executive has
facts and studies upon which to make a reasonable judgment. It is no
longer a decision based on an enthusiastic proposal.

Phase Three: Once approved, the product enters Phase 3: full-scale
development, including final design and manufacture, cost, pricing, pro-

Figure 2-5

Company Objectives

Phase 1
Preliminary Study
Product Committee

Sales & Mkt
Prelim. Mkt
Estimate

Engineering
Feasibility
Limiting Factors

Phase 2
Intermediate Study
Product Committee

Sales & Mkt
Distribution
Forecasts
Market needs

Administration
Accounting
Legal Questions
Personnel
Profitability

Manufacturing
Facilities
Mfg Cost
Mtl Problems

Engineering
Pattern Dwg.
Prelim Designs
Tool Needs
Facilities

Phase 3
Decision to Proceed
President

Sales & Mkt
Identify Cust
Pricing
Training
Adv & Prom

Administration
Cost Methods
Allocations
Profit Estimates
Payment Terms

Manufacturing
Assign Equip
Assign Space
Value Mfg
Produce

Engineering
Final Designs
Standards
Value Engr

Phase 4
Launch

Phase 5
Follow up

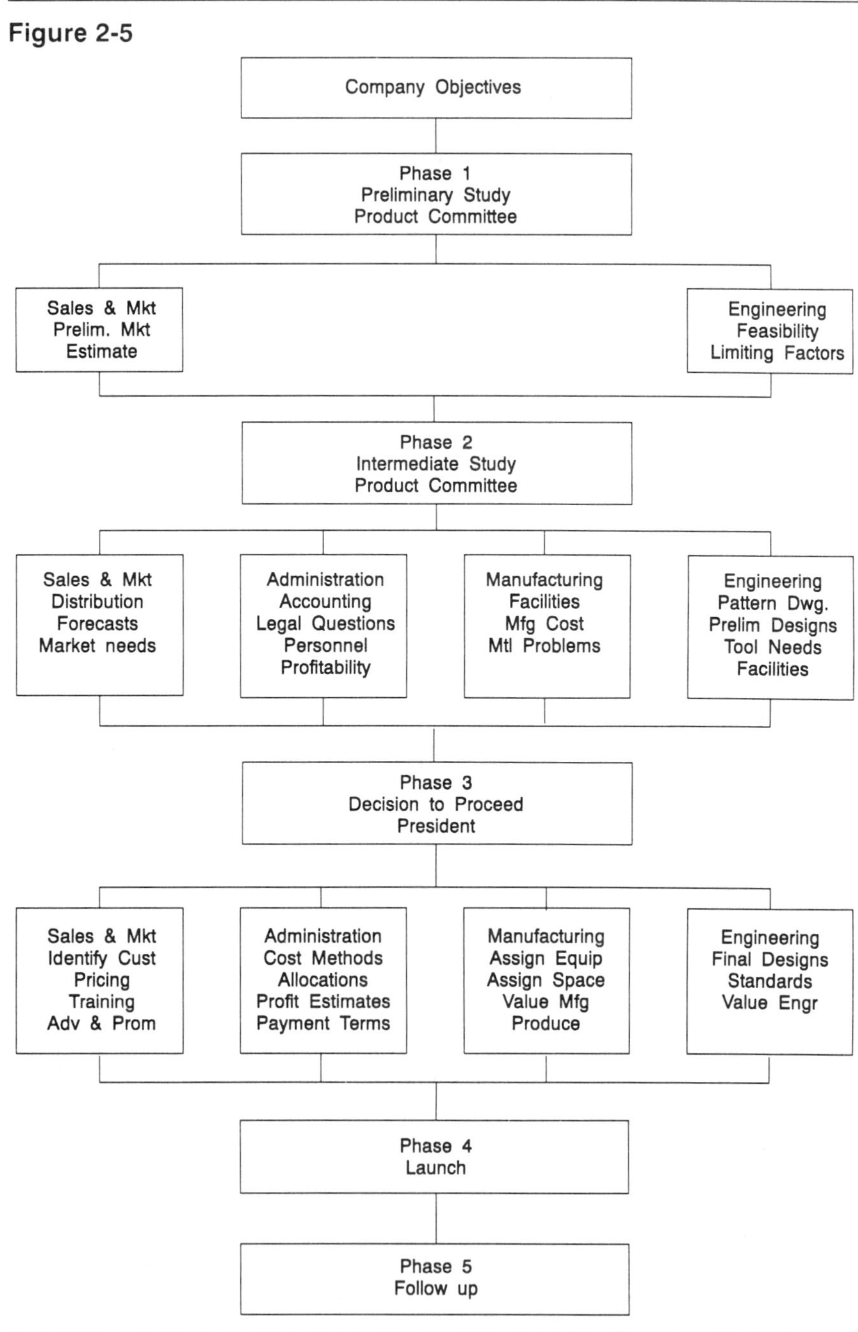

motion, sales training, and profit determinations. This involves a full commitment to proceed and spend the approved funds. By this time, all the proper people are involved and have the opportunity to express either positive or negative recommendations. With all this background, the project can proceed, presumably without too many surprises. There always will be unforeseen situations, but this procedure should reduce them to a minimum.

Phase Four: This step involves the product "launch." If it is a revolutionary new product, the performance and capabilities would have been kept secret up to this time. It may require that test units be placed in some good customers' plants as "beta" test sites. In such situations, customers operate the products under regular service conditions, rather than in laboratory, controlled installations. These tests may highlight necessary modifications to correct problems or to make the product more acceptable. If the product is not "new to the world" but merely an addition to the line, the intense secrecy is not as significant.

Now the industrial press can be notified and the units sold to all customers. Marketing and sales must give demonstrations and invite customers into the factory to see the product manufactured and demonstrated. This introductory stage of the product life cycle requires convincing arguments to customers who may be spending significant sums on installations. These people do not want to buy untested, unsure products for service in critical processes in their plants.

Phase Five: This involves product follow-up and reevaluation. Not all products perform well, even after intensive preliminary review. Unfortunately, improper assumptions can be made about the size of the market, the real needs of customers, pricing, or the durability of the product in actual operation. This does not obviate the need for the screening process. It merely confirms that the various steps must be carried out carefully.

PROBLEM AREAS

Companies introduce new products for various reasons, not all of them valid. Despite screening processes, senior managers sometimes take on new products because they fit the manufacturing capability or because an enterprising inventor "sold" them well. When senior managers are the "champions" of new products, it is difficult to point out the negative factors that influence customer acceptance.

Similarly, there may be a reluctance to abandon certain products. Thus, many companies retain products that may have passed their useful life and are well into the decline phase of their product life cycle. There is a feeling that the product has served the company well in its better days, coupled with a reluctance to admit that those "good old days" are over. A product that was the brainchild of a senior official of the company becomes doubly difficult to abandon. Often the sales force will fight the deletion of a product on the basis that it gives them less to sell. These invalid reasons must yield to good product management.

SUCCESS RATES

The success rate for new products is elusive. Years ago, certain new products failed because their originators failed to do their homework. By ignoring the early steps in the process, they wasted millions of dollars. However, the reader must always recognize the difference in definitions of success in new product introductions. The Conference Board declares a new product successful "if it met management's original expectations for it in all important respects." Conversely, a major new product is considered a failure if "in some important respect, it failed to have met management's original expectations for it."[4] With these definitions, the Conference Board study of 1980 reported little difference in success rates between 1971 and 1979. However, the Conference Board's surveys cover only those products actually brought to market. Other surveys may describe as failures those products that were discarded in the early stages when market research or technology may have forestalled introduction.

New product failures can have many causes. They include, but are not limited to, a lack of customer need, faulty market research, technical problems, and poor timing. However, there is some question concerning when and how to measure product failure. If the product success or failure is dated from the original concept, it will present a far different picture than if measured from the commercialization date. The reader must take a cautious approach to failure rates unsupported by a stated measurement date.

SUMMARY

The product is obviously a major factor in the marketing mix. While industrial products, like consumer products, can be called "groups of values" or satisfactions, they differ materially in their applications, numbers and types of customers, values, distribution, and organization. This book uses capital goods as its basis for discussion and related solutions.

The market is large in dollars, but small in numbers of potential customers, if compared to the consumer industry. Well-defined industries provide for relatively good statistics. Comparisons within the industries as to size and growth are, therefore, possible.

The product manager should enjoy a strong position in the industrial organization. They often are fully responsible for their products, even to the point of profit. They must know their markets, pricing, and competition and must be able to manage their organizations in cooperation with the other functions.

Although the rest of the firm may adopt matrix organizations, product managers are responsible for their products no matter what the application or end-use. To prevent biasing all decisions in one direction, committees should be established to review products.

Current products are usually the mainstay of the company. They provide sales and profits, and give a consistency and continuity to the firm. Strong efforts continue to maintain or improve present product positions through active marketing. If some erosion takes place, there are steps that might reverse that trend. If these steps fail, it may be necessary to discard or sell off a product line. This may result in some unrest or morale problems within the company. There are always emotional attachments to products, and people do not like to see them abandoned.

New products provide an infusion of new enthusiasm and new life to a company. There is always risk of failure involved, and this may be observed at management and operating levels. However, there is also risk in not developing new products—the risk of missing profitable opportunities.

Failure rates of new products vary with the source of information. If measured from the first concept generated, the rate will be much different from that measured after market launch. When considering this question, always be sure of the measurement terms. It may reduce hesitation.

Product abandonment is often painful, akin to losing an old friend. There are times when it is necessary, and these occasions should be faced. Deferring the decision too long may penalize profits severely.

REFERENCES

1. United States, *Survey of Current Business*, January 1989, U.S. Department of Commerce.

2. Pride, William M., and Ferrell, O.C., *Marketing: Basic Concepts and Strategies*, 7th ed., Boston, MA: Houghton Mifflin Company, 1991, p. 249. Used with permission.
3. Crawford, Merle C., *New Products Management*, 3rd ed. Homewood, IL: Richard D. Irwin Inc., 1991, pp. 35-36.
4. Hopkins, David, *New Product Winners and Losers* (Report No. 773), New York, NY: The Conference Board, 1980, p. 4.

3

Competition

nformation on competition is essential for successful combat in the marketplace. Knowledge of competitors' strengths and weaknesses permits a company to formulate plans and strategies. It is important to recognize that market strengths are not limited to the vagaries of the economy. The following are important in any analysis:

- The reasons to study competition;

- The types of information that all companies should have about their competitors;

- Sources of competitive information that are easy to tap;

- Who makes the analysis and how it can be reported; and

- The need for continuing analysis.

Competitive information is vital to all organizations. Do you know your competitors? Do you know their sales and profits? Do you know their likely reactions to your activities? How would you go about answering these questions? The information is critical to your operations. An intuitive knowledge of certain companies is difficult to translate to broad levels.

The Conference Board defines competitive intelligence as:

> "... both the product and the process of collecting various kinds of data thought to be relevant—anything from trade rumors and financial statistics to product specifications and news of plant construction—and then selecting, interpreting, and presenting the data to be used in decision making."[1]

While a competitor may not operate in precisely the same industry, it may compete for the same consumer dollar. For example, a steel company may compete with a plastics manufacturer. Substitution of material crosses industry lines and does not respect prior customs. However, in this chapter we will deal with direct competitors functioning in the same industry. Since they make the same type of products, they can be considered competitors in the truest sense.

WHY STUDY COMPETITION?

The significant needs that motivate a company to know more about its competition and its industry are:

- To **know the opposition;**
- To measure the **size of the industry;**
- To know the **composition of the industry;**
- To **develop strategy** for the marketplace; and
- To **determine competitive response.**

The Need to Know the Opposition

Just as an athletic team must scout the teams it plays, so must a business firm scout its competitors. Visualize an athletic team that has never studied its opponents' strengths or weaknesses, offensive power, or defensive abilities. This type of team will take to the field facing a tremendous and unnecessary disadvantage. The same philosophy applies in business: it's extremely unwise to enter the market without knowing the opposition.

The Need to Measure the Size of the Industry

If the competition cannot be identified, it is almost impossible to gauge the size of the industry or to judge whether one is earning a reasonable market share. If a firm's sales rose 10 percent from one year to the next, it might be assumed a healthy growth. However, if industry sales rose 25 percent, then the subject company would be in a comparative decline. Only a responsible competitive analysis can establish the size, make-up and performance of an industry.

The Need to Know the Make-up of the Industry

To know the **total size** of an industry is not enough. It is equally important to know its **make-up.** If competitors are delivering new products, a firm that is not conscious of this fact may be caught unaware and fall behind. The knowledge of competition is necessary for survival. While competition, in the theoretical marketing sense, is uncontrollable, this does not mean it should be ignored, nor that nothing can be done about it. For survival, one must know the make-up of an industry, including size, type, and movement of individual competitors.

Strategy in the Marketplace

Competitive knowledge also decides your own company strategy in the marketplace. One strategy may be used if your firm is a price leader, another if your company is small and insignificant, still another when considering factors such as service and reputation. This process should be planned, not reactive.

Competitive Response

Competitive intelligence determines how rivals might respond to our actions. Correct discernment helps answer questions such as:

- What will the competition do if we introduce a revolutionary new product? Will they play it down or copy it?

- What will the competition do if we adjust prices?

- What will the competition do if we change distribution channels?

- What will the competition do if we mount strong advertising and public relations campaigns to improve company or product image?

The above factors only begin to portray the need to learn more about competition than most companies generally know. To remain strong, or grow stronger, companies must know as much as possible about their adversaries.

The degree of sophistication of competitive analysis will vary by company and by industry. A small firm need not be super-sophisticated. In most companies, the sales manager will know intuitively some of the competition and will have a feel for the relevant **qualitative** information. For a small company, these data may suffice. However, for a larger company, it is necessary to apply this information to a total program. The larger the company and the larger and more complex the industry, the more essential it is that **intuition be replaced with a total, integrated program** of competitive analysis. It is necessary to know all competitors and to anticipate the industry's reaction to product innovation, new pricing policies, and the like, from each specific company.

ESSENTIAL INFORMATION

Up to this point, we have concentrated on the importance of competitive analysis. We can conclude that it is: (a) extremely important, and (b) not necessarily highly structured. The following summarizes the key facts that a company should know about its competition. In order to bring a competing company into focus, these questions should be answered:

1. **History**

    - How did the company start?

    - Where is it in its life cycle?

    - What other companies has it either bought or divested?

2. **Ownership**

    The personality, philosophy, and likely course of action of a firm may depend on its ownership.

- Is it a public company? Are there dominant stockholders?

- Is it a division or subsidiary of a multinational or giant corporation? Is it foreign or domestic owned?

3. Products

- Are the product lines directly comparable to our own, or are only some of them competitive? (This is necessary to know when making comparisons with published data.)

- Is the competitive product line full range or line limited?

- Does the competitor frequently introduce new products, or has the product line remained unchanged for some time?

- Are the products acceptable to the marketplace?

4. Strengths

- Is the competition strong in reputation, pricing policy, product superiority, service after sale, engineering capability, and the like?

5. Competitive position

- How large is the industry?

- Who makes up the industry?

- What is the relative size of each competitor and what is its market share?

- Has any competitor increased its market share over the years or just recently?

- Has any competitor consistently maintained the same market share as the market rose and declined?

6. Plans and strategies

These are difficult areas to research, particularly with reference to new products and new markets. Knowing a competitor's past performance is valuable, but even more valuable is an estimate of what it will do in the future.

- How does it react to other companies?

- Is it a product and market leader or a follower?

- Can you determine its goals?

7. Problems

Salespeople often give the impression that competitors are superior in price, delivery, performance, and new products. On the contrary, competitors also have their problems. To operate properly in the marketplace, a company must remain aware of its competitors' problems.

- Have competitors' products performed as expected?

- Have there been strikes or labor unrest?

- Have fires, floods, or other phenomena reduced production, reducing sales and profits?

8. Facilities

- What of the production and office facilities? Are they new and efficient, or old and ineffective?

- Are the present properties landlocked where no building expansion is possible? (If so, they might require an entirely new plant.)

- Which competitors have the latest equipment to ensure quality control, including machining and measuring?

9. Management and quality of personnel

An organization is more than bricks, mortar, and machine tools. The quality of its leadership is crucial to the organization's strength.

- Have the same people guided the competitors for years? If so, the path to the present may indicate the direction of the future.

- Has a new management team come from the outside, giving no signals as to what the future may bring?

- Is top management innovative or the type only to modify products already on the market?

- Are other personnel—sales, manufacturing, R&D, engineering, and others—aggressive and progressive?

10. Range of activity

Competitive strengths and weaknesses often show in information gleaned from other parts of the world. A global range gives any company the advantage of experimentally marketing new products elsewhere.

♦ Are the competitors global or local?

11. Financial strength

♦ Are competitors using too much "creative accounting"?

♦ Have their profits matched ours or the industry's?

Various financial ratios can compare a competitor with one's own performance or the industry as a whole. A discussion of this process follows later in this chapter.

12. Industry leadership

♦ Which competitor is the industry leader in price, service, innovation, and new product development?

♦ Which competitors are followers, copying product lines and market approaches? Imitation versus innovation is a popular topic. Although few like to admit they are derivative, some successful companies have practiced this strategy.

13. Organizational changes

♦ What recent organizational changes have competitors initiated?

♦ What precipitated these changes—mergers or acquisitions or poor performance?

Management shifts may signal new strengths or direction. Just as changes in one's physical well-being may signal medical problems, competitor management changes often signal shifts in organizational health.

14. Litigation

♦ Are competitors involved in legal battles with other companies or with the government?

♦ If so, does the litigation center on alleged price fixing, discrimination, illegal payoff, safety, consumerism, or some other legal issue? Knowledge of competitors' trials provides insight to their problems and may forewarn one's own company of possible similar suits in the offing.

While this list is not comprehensive, it does suggest that knowledge of these factors can improve the decision-making capabilities of most companies dramatically. However, defining what one would like to know about competition is easier than gathering the facts and interpreting them.

INFORMATION SOURCES

Following are some available information sources, with suggested techniques for unearthing more-obscure data. Good business libraries will contain most of these references.

The Standard Industrial Classification (SIC)

This is a code by which the U.S. government classifies all establishments by their principal lines of business.[2] This is a useful, common designation that refers to several of the following sources. A two-digit code identifies the basic industry; for example, 20 designates the food industry, and 26 designates the paper industry. These codes are subdivided into three- to seven-digit codes, each a further refinement of the initial two-digit code. The following example will illustrate:

20	Food
201	Meat Products
2011	Meat Packing Plants
20117	Luncheon meats from meatpacking plants
20117x	(Undefined)
2011717	Dry or semi-dry meats (e.g. salami)

Since each establishment has a code (and not just the total company), it is possible to identify the principal product or output of any facility. In other words, all General Electric Company is not classified under electric products. The GE plants that produce turbines are classed accordingly. When submitting their tax and census reports, all companies must list their SIC codes. The value of this tool is obvious. Since a common set of codes classifies all manufacturers, those firms in any industry can be pinpointed by state and county. Therefore, one can locate lesser known competitors in any field.

General Sources of Information

Considered to be obvious, these are often overlooked. These include *The Wall Street Journal, Fortune, Forbes, Business Week*, and many other business publications that report company activities. Like government intelligence, commercial intelligence consists of amassing insignificant-appearing information into a central whole to tell a compelling story.

Letters From the Field Sales Force

These communiques report on the status and outcome of various negotiations. The letters may be haphazard, arrive irregularly, and may not cover all jobs and all markets. However, they are an excellent source of **primary** information from the marketplace. These may be far more significant than the secondary sources described later.

Call Reports

These are often fertile sources of information. Salespeople tend to dislike call reports, which are not always complete and sometimes not even truthful. However, call reports may verify that a particular competitor is working harder in a certain territory, perhaps by cutting prices or advertising heavily. This primary information would be very expensive to collect by sending interviewers to all customers. (See Chapter 6 on call reports.)

Clipping Services From Local Newspapers

Newspapers in the competitors' cities often report articles of a social but not business interest, e.g., "John Jones married Mary Smith." But they also report plant expansions, new hiring, restructurings, and other changes in personnel—news that does not receive national coverage but provides valuable insights.

Customers

Customers often provide interesting news of competitors during normal conversation, without probing. During the quotation stage or after job awards, one may ask the customer the names of the bidders and how they compared in the negotiation. Often this information comes unsolicited. For example, a customer may try to get a better price or performance by asking the salesperson to match an offering of a competitor.

Many companies, as part of their regular forecasting procedure, ask their salespeople to review next year's requirements with their customers. That may be a good time to discuss not only the total requirements but also the percentage expected, thus revealing the business going to others.

Brokerage Studies

Such studies on individual companies are usually more informative than annual reports, newspapers, or other generally available sources. These studies frequently report the company sales by individual product or industry. Besides listing orders, shipments, and profits, they often estimate these criteria for the future. Further, such studies report present strengths and weaknesses and what corrective steps may be underway. *The Wall Street Journal* usually carries lists of the newly available studies. Letters of request to the brokerage houses often go unanswered. However, the *Wall Street Transcript* (not related to *The Wall Street Journal*) usually carries reports of financial analysts' meetings with corporate executives that give similar detailed information not contained elsewhere.

The 10K Reports

These are extremely valuable sources of information. This report must be submitted to the Securities and Exchange Commission within 90 days following the close of the fiscal year. It provides some history, a list of products and their relative importance, references to competition, and percentage of sales to the user industries. The 10K also discusses new products and current litigation. Income statements, balance sheets, and other financial schedules are required. Also, the reports list total advertising outlays, and total research and development expense. These can signal changes in promotion or development that reflect a new approach to the market. The 10K reports are available from the reporting companies upon request.

Company Employees

Present employees are an excellent information source. Gathering the product and industry specialists into a brainstorming session provides a forum for wide-ranging discussion. A display of charts and graphs can inform these people of the present knowledge with a request to build upon it. Combining these opinions furnishes a clearer profile of the individual competitor and the industry as a whole. Brainstorming sessions elicit many points of view from different locations, providing a more well-rounded picture than individual discussions.

Industrial Directories

The *Thomas Register* and other industrial directories are valuable sources of names of competitors. With the product lines listed alphabetically, you can compile a list of other sellers or producers in your product areas. In addition, one section of the *Thomas Register* provides catalog information. Other directories worth reviewing include Moody's *Industrial Manual* and Standard and Poor's *Register of Corporations*, publications of a financial nature that also contain other useful facts.

Most states publish directories listing resident firms alphabetically, geographically, and by industry. Each listing customarily shows products manufactured, SIC, and the number of employees. Since this list is by facility, it shows the number of employees at each location.

Annual Reports

Primarily directed to stockholders, they have a goal of providing a favorable image to investors and the public. Though not as valuable as the 10K for details, they do contain helpful data. It is worthwhile to review both documents. They are available from the reporting companies or in good business libraries.

Dun & Bradstreet Reports

These reports detail the individual directors' backgrounds and present financial analyses of the health and strength of the companies reviewed. These reports have the reputation of accurate, impartial studies. The *Million Dollar* and *Half Million Dollar* directories published by Dun & Bradstreet may be used to confirm total sales or total employee figures found elsewhere.

Government Reports

Many reports are issued by federal, state, and local governments. Such reports may show industry and plant size by area. Although federal census reports do not name companies, knowledge of industry location in various counties can help pinpoint information on employee levels for firms under study. Federal government reports on other countries list imports and exports by product line. In addition, the Census Bureau and other government services make worldwide estimates of sales of certain products. The *Census of Manufacturers* lists total sales and employment by industry code, providing a measure of the total industry size within the United States. Many other useful reports are available at reasonable cost from the government. The local Department of Commerce office can help locate available information and refer the researcher to other likely sources.

Purchased Lists

Organizations such as Dun & Bradstreet, Chilton Publishing, and Economic Information Services provide purchased lists by SIC numbers. Some contain data such as total sales, number of employees, name of chief operating officer, and the like. One can obtain a list of companies in industry 3822 (instruments) as a tabulation, computer tape, deck of cards, or computer access. This list would show all companies manufacturing instruments in code 3822. Admittedly, some of these lists are imperfect. Someone familiar with the industry must sort out the information. However, such lists can provide valuable information not available elsewhere.

MAKING THE ANALYSIS

Having gathered this information, it now becomes a question of how to handle it. Initially a file must be created for individual competitors. One problem will be keeping too much information, some of it valueless. The files must be kept meaningful, or they become too unwieldy. It is also essential to keep files up to date.

This material resides in different departments in different companies—some in sales, some in market research, and others in corporate. In any case, one person should be charged with the overall responsibility. This may be added to other duties or may function as a full time position, depending on the emphasis the company places on this activity.

REPORTING

As a new function, the researcher may want to provide immediate output. This is helpful feedback to field sales if they have been primary sources for the information. In this case, a brief newsletter is valuable. It can be a **summary** of the latest reports from the field or published sources. It can be a **brief single report** on one competitor. The output is quick, need not be formal, and will encourage additional input from the field. It would be a good idea to have the output in a standard format for the readers to recognize every issue as a flash report.

Eventually, a more formal set of reports should be generated. One company should be selected for the first detailed analysis. At this point, identify your audience. Write for your readers. If the report is for financial management, include more financial analyses. If it is for the field, couch the analysis from their viewpoint. If it is for general management, write it from their perspective. Some will read the reports only for general information, others as a guide to the direction of certain competitors. Assemble the report in a consistent format that will lead the reader through the competitor's organization; avoid presenting a jumble of disorganized facts. With a standardized form, all competitors can be analyzed on the same basis and among themselves.

REPORT TOPICS

The following outline suggests some topics and their content:

- Name and history of the firm;
- Products and structure (by industry, product, area);
- Charts and tables;
- Evaluation;
- International activities; and
- Appendix.

Name and History of the Firm

This first section includes the official name of the company, which may have changed several times since its founding. Also include a brief history of the firm. The history should contain a list of the acquisitions and divestitures to clarify the company size and make-up. Given the complexity of many multinational firms today, such a history may be long but necessary to focus on significant changes.

Products and Structure

A company defined on a product output basis generally is easier to study than one defined on a functional or geographical basis. The products should be detailed for type and size, particularly if holes exist in the line. If there are product divisions, each may stand alone as a separate profit center. This is advantageous in analysis, especially if your products do not compete with all their divisions.

Many companies organize by industry. Here the industry divisions may be the profit centers. If your company is organized on the same basis, that is fine. But if you are organized by product with somewhat different lines, comparisons become more difficult. Geographic comparisons become clouded with either product or industry organizations.

Charts and Tables

This section can present a wealth of information in very few pages. Charts and tables should be used to compare competition with your performance. These charts would include, among other data, net sales, pretax profit, orders, backlog, etc. Figure 3-1 illustrates the general format of the net sales comparison, and Figure 3-2 reviews industry comparisons. Figure 3-3 compares branch office locations.

A ratio analysis displays how well the competitor operated within the boundaries of the normal ratios such as pretax profit as a percent of sales. Figure 3-4 illustrates this approach. Dun & Bradstreet publishes industry financial ratios annually. Merely charting the history of the competition is not adequate, since the question "Compared to what?" constantly arises. The next section addresses this matter.

Evaluation

This section builds on the charts and tables. Do not leave all interpretation to the reader, since the reader will not posses the depth of information collected by the preparer. Among other phenomena, acquisitions, major strikes, floods, and the like affect the performance in ways the researcher

Figure 3-1 Net Sales—Historical Pattern

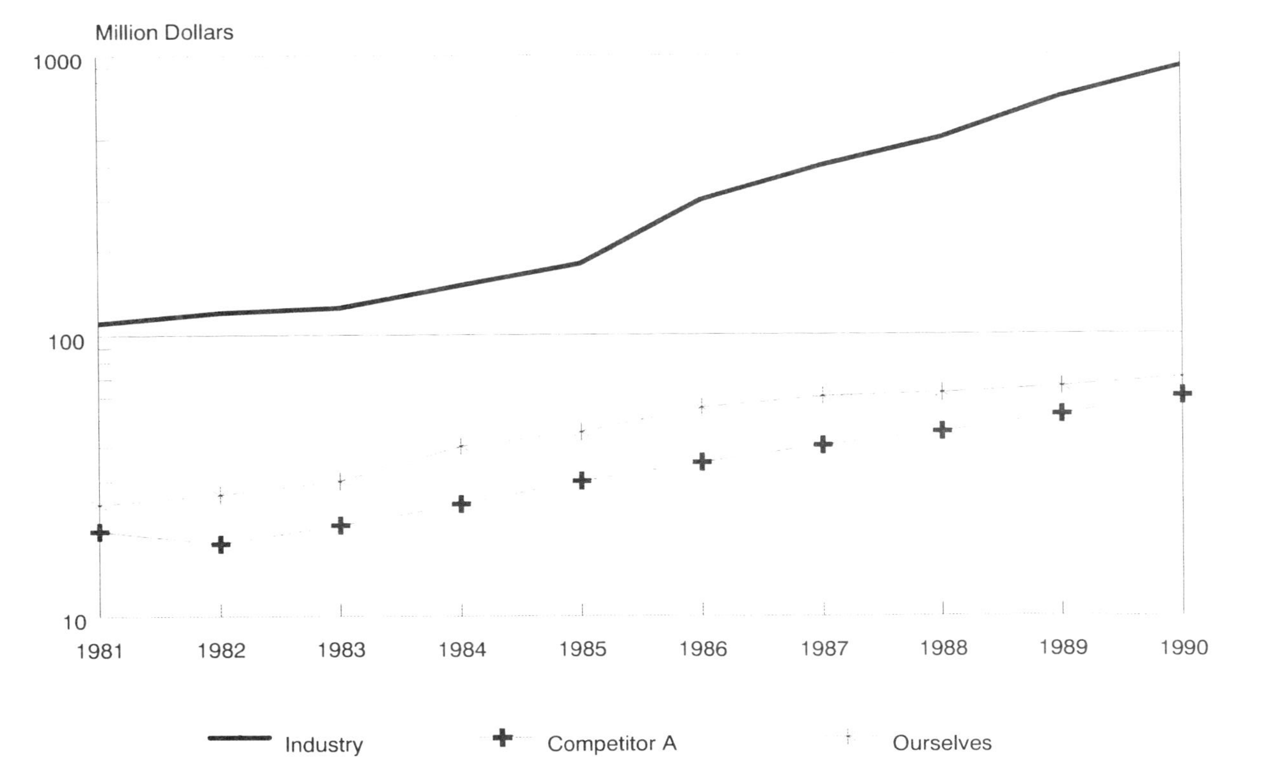

**Figure 3-2 Industry Statistics—Comparison with Competitor A
In Million $**

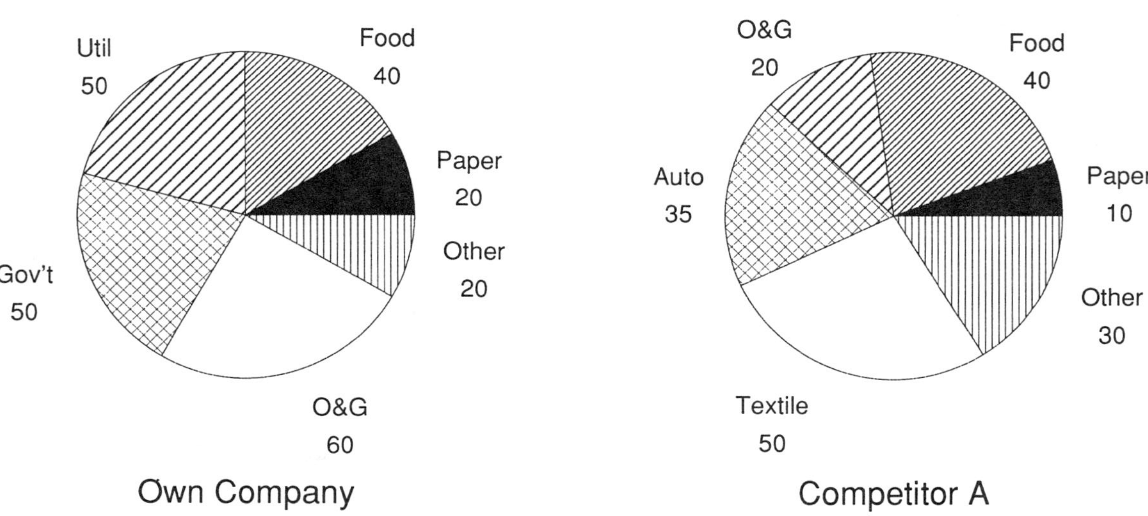

Figure 3-3

PRODUCT ORDERS BY BRANCH

OFFICE	Our Own	COMPETITOR A	COMPETITOR B
Boston	X	X	X
New York	X	X	X
Philadelphia	X	X	X
Washington		X	X
Charlotte	X		
Atlanta	X	X	
Pittsburgh	X	X	X
Cincinnati		X	
Detroit	X	X	X
Cleveland	X	X	
Chicago	X	X	X
Kansas City			X
Houston	X	X	
Tulsa	X		
New Orleans		X	
Denver		X	
San Francisco	X	X	X
Seattle	X	X	X
Los Angeles	X	X	X

Figure 3-4 Ratios—Pretax Profit/Net Sales—Competitor A

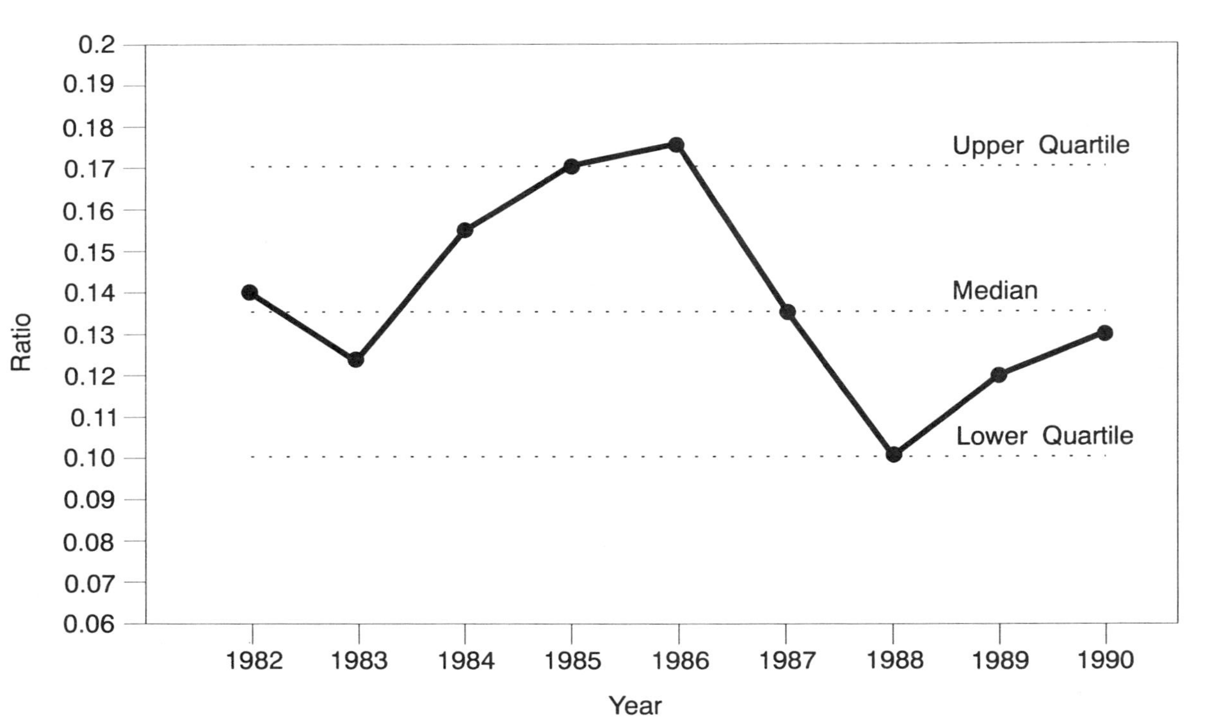

will recognize. However, the casual reader may not be aware of these factors and may make incorrect assumptions from the plotted data.

The interpretation and evaluation, therefore, should list any qualifications in the data: estimated material, whatever weaknesses exist in the data, whether it includes more than one product, and any other significant limitations. It is difficult to interpret these charts and tables fully, since the information available to the researcher may be limited. Therefore, expressions such as "it appears that" or "the data seem to imply" show that interpretation is of good, but not necessarily complete, information.

International Activities

An understanding of a competitor's activities beyond the United States can be useful. Some companies operate only domestically; others have offices in other countries, and others are truly global. Some foreign operations may have different names than the parent company, thus obscuring the relationship. Sometimes competitors have great strength in one or a few countries but not throughout the world. New products may be introduced and market tested in other countries before final release in the United States. International operations should be a part of the total profile.

Appendix

The appendix contains supplementary charts and tables used for reference early in the report and can be interpreted at leisure by the reader. In addition, catalogs of the competitor may be included here. The appendix also should contain a listing of the officers and directors and a list of plant facilities. Supplementary material fills in the picture drawn by the report and is useful as a springboard to additional analysis, if required.

CONTINUING ANALYSIS REQUIRED

It is not enough to prepare these detailed reports and then file them as a completed project. Such analyses and reviews must be updated continually, since the marketplace is extremely dynamic. The philosophy of a competitor may change quickly due to a change in ownership or management. To ensure that radical changes don't occur unnoticed, continual review is imperative. Reviews and updates of prior reports can accompany preparation of new reports on other competitors. Establish a process of continual review of the entire market and the individuals who make up that market. If the size of the market has been relatively constant and one competitor now appears to be taking a larger share of that market, another must be losing share. This kind of information is pertinent, because it highlights shifts in power.

SUMMARY

Competitive studies are necessary to know and measure the industry and its make-up. With this information, one can develop a strategy for the marketplace and prepare for the competition's response.

Many kinds of information are important in these studies. Not all of what you would like to know is readily available. However, by gathering as much as possible many unknown pieces will fall into place. Some of this likely will be discarded later. At this point, it may be difficult to separate the essential from the unimportant.

The sources, as presented here, are many. The field sales force and home office people as primary sources should be contacted first. In some cases, they may have to get back to you on specific points of interest. They become basic points of input and therefore must be fed output promptly.

Business libraries are excellent sources of secondary data. Their reference material on domestic and foreign companies will help immeasureably. The ability to use a computer to search for this material has made the process much simpler. Microfilm or microfiche files may contain the 10K reports of your study companies. Also, many federal government reports may be on file here.

A responsible individual or team must be assigned. All types of competitive information should funnel through this department. Files should be set up and culled for extraneous material. A system for continuous update and review should be installed. The method of filing will depend on the company. Some will have almost everything computerized; others may use manual filing.

Reporting should be prompt. Distribution lists require some decisions. Your guideline must be to decide who has the "need to know."

Finally, follow up the initial reports with continuing updates. Knowing what you knew last year is not enough. Keeping current with your knowledge of your opposition is essential.

REFERENCES

1. Sutton, Howard, *Competitive Intelligence* (Research Report No. 913), New York, NY: The Conference Board, 1988, p. vii.
2. United States, Office of Management and Budget, *Standard Industrial Classification Manual*, Washington, D.C., 1987.

4

Distribution Channels

Marketing channels provide the interface between producer and the industrial consumer. Mutual communication and confidence are essential for continuing relationships. Understanding the alternatives fosters continuing review. Though sometimes difficult to change, channels are not always permanent. The following factors should be considered.

- The available paths to the customer: direct and indirect;
- Advantages and disadvantages of available distribution institutions;
- Factors for consideration when reviewing channels; and
- Evaluation of present versus prospective channels.

The distribution channel is the link between the manufacturer and customer. While there can be several different paths within a channel, the principal categories, as illustrated in Figure 4-1, are:

♦ Direct distribution, where the producer sells to the customer through its own sales force;

♦ Indirect distribution, in which the manufacturer sells through intermediaries: manufacturers' representatives (reps), distributors, or a combination of the two; and

♦ Multiple channels, with direct sales offices in some areas or for some industries and indirect offices for the remainder.

Since no single channel is ideal for all companies or all conditions, the advantages and disadvantages of both systems will be explored. The needs may change due to changes in product line, life cycle stage, competitive pressures, and efforts to reduce selling costs. Since marketing is a dynamic activity, expect that changes will occur over time.

Figure 4-1

POSSIBLE CHANNELS
FOR INDUSTRIAL PRODUCTS

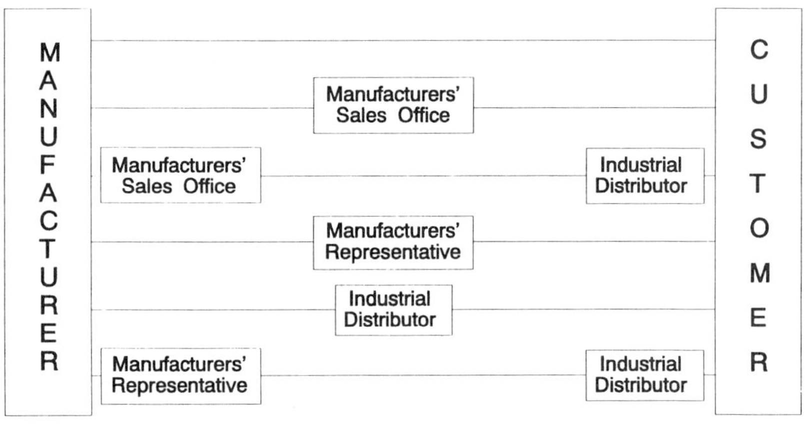

DIRECT PATHS

Direct channels can follow one of two paths:

1. From the producer directly to the customer; and

2. From the producer through the manufacturer's own sales offices.

The former is the shortest industrial channel and is used where there are a limited number of customers. The other direct channel, through manufacturers' sales offices, can accommodate greater numbers of final customers while providing for complete control. For the purposes of this work, these will be considered as one, namely, a channel strategy that does not use intermediaries. The term "intermediary" is now the preferred choice for the previous designation, "middleman."

When the producer sells through its own sales branches to industrial distributors, it retains control over the first part of the process but loses control at the distributor-customer transaction. It does give manufacturers' sales offices wider customer coverage, as well as the ability to relinquish the small orders to organizations particularly qualified for this activity.

INDIRECT PATHS

Indirect channels may take several paths due to various combinations of intermediaries.

- ◆ **Producer to Manufacturers' Representatives to Customer:** These reps normally do not stock products but serve as company salespeople. While they can be very effective, they do not allow as much control by the principal. Normally they function as the customer contacts, accepting orders and placing them with the producers. They accept orders and bill in their own names. The producer bills the reps at a discounted net price, the difference between list and net resulting in the rep's profit or commission.

- ◆ **Producer to Distributor to Customer:** This gives the manufacturer the benefit of wide customer coverage, with stocking sources near the customers. This is a popular method, even though it limits control by the producer. Here, too, the distributor accepts orders in his own name, and gains his commission as the difference between the customer price and his own cost from the producer.

- ◆ **Producer to Rep to Distributor to Customer:** This offers benefits similar to those available when sales offices sell through distributors, and is used in territories requiring wide coverage, but with insufficient potential to justify a direct sales office. Note that even in indirect channels, company sales offices may be involved. Figure 4-1 illustrates the usual combinations.

The actual process of channel strategy may include several of these combinations. Dual distribution, multichannel, and hybrid systems are terms that describe this phenomenon. The challenge for the marketer is to design and operate a channel system that minimizes cost and maximizes customer coverage. While there is no one answer for all companies, the following remarks will help managers or analysts to arrive at a meaningful evaluation based upon their specific requirements.

CHANNEL MANAGEMENT

Management of the channels will depend upon the path the producer's management selects. A central sales executive typically manages direct channels, which are subdivided into local territories controlled by branch managers. With rep organizations, the central sales management directs operations from the home office. Where distributors exist, a home office distributor sales manager is likely to be in place, to select, train, and generally oversee distributor activities. If the distributors report to branch offices, branch managers probably will retain at least advisory control. However, responsibility ultimately resides with the distributor sales manager.

Cost Versus Control

In selecting channels, there are usually trade-offs between cost and control. Selling through manufacturers' sales branches may result in an expense-to-orders ratio of about 10 percent. A good part of this will be fixed cost. Selling through reps, distributors, or both may cost the producer up to 20 percent to 25 percent in commissions, with less control. However, this is not a fixed cost, and may finally result in better coverage and lower cost in sparse territories or where the intermediaries have special expertise. Therefore, analyzing dollar cost alone will not provide the full answer.

DIRECT CHANNELS (Advantages and Disadvantages)

A primary advantage of a direct channel is the control it provides. With one's own sales force, individual salespeople can be directed to carry out certain activities. As company employees, they must comply with company directives. This is important if the company wants to use the sales force to collect market information or to do missionary work in quest of new customers. It is also valuable in supplying complete information on orders and customers. This information is not always available from intermediaries.

A major disadvantage with direct distribution is the built-in fixed cost. Maintaining a field sales organization involves a relatively constant cost, (assuming fixed salaries and office expenses), even as orders fluctuate. In other words, when staffing remains unchanged, expenses also remain the same even if orders drop. In an indirect organization, commissions relate to orders, and reductions in orders translate into reduced selling expense. Further, it takes considerable time and investment to build and maintain a direct sales force. Locating and training good sales people are challenging assignments.

INDIRECT CHANNELS (Manufacturers' Representatives)

Manufacturers' representatives (reps) are salespeople who represent several companies and handle noncompeting but complementary products in specific geographic areas. Reps may or may not take title to the goods sold. Although the typical agreement calls for the producer to bill the intermediary, there are customers who insist on placing the orders with, and receiving billing from, the producers. This may reflect either the size of the order or a higher level of customer confidence in the producer. Such customers may believe the rep is not financially equipped to handle very large contracts.

Reps work under contractual agreements that have a normal termination period of 90 days. A written agreement normally spells out details such as length of contract, products covered, commission structure, territory covered and pricing authority. The intermediary ordinarily maintains only limited control over prices and terms of payment. Sometimes the producers must authorize competitive discounts. This raises the question of who absorbs the reduction in income, the producer or the intermediary. The custom is to negotiate this problem, with both parties typically sharing the income reduction.

Reps can be useful if:

♦ The territory will not support a direct sales office;

♦ Overload is a direct sales force problem;

♦ The producer is not well known in the area; and

♦ A product line has limits.

With reps in the picture, the producer's investment is minimal. Moreover, reps can sell to small market segments not covered by a direct sales force. Sometimes reps have better relationships with customers, because they sell several products and thus are in more frequent contact with buyers.

However, there can be disadvantages to the use of intermediaries. Since they represent several principals, their commitment can be fragmented. Further, reps may not follow up on leads and inquiries as rapidly as desired. Getting reports on lost orders or on customer activities may be difficult. Loyalty to the producer may be lacking.

INDIRECT CHANNELS (Distributors)

Distributors are independent firms, usually small, which normally sell, stock, and take title to the products. Since they usually represent several manufacturers, they can offer complete lines. Some may specialize in complete lines such as power transmission equipment, stocking and selling gears, industrial chain, couplings, drive belts, conveyors, and the like.

Distributors permit the manufacturer to profit from the elimination of small orders that can be expensive to support. Distributors who are specialists in certain lines may offer additional services to the customer such as installation and repair. This works well with standardized products that require little technical support. Also, some customers prefer dealing with local distributors.

Conversely, certain advantages can be nullified by factors such as lack of technical knowledge on the distributor's part, the loss of distributors when products are not selling well, lack of control over the selling effort, or a distributor's tendency to concentrate on the most profitable lines. Further, distributors consider their customer lists as part of their stock-in-trade and are reluctant to share this data with the producers. Often the producers do not know which customers or industries bought the products that were sold through distributors.

Resellers appear to be making increasing contributions to the channels according to recent statistics. Although some observers believe the trend favors the direct approach, there are indications that indirect channels are growing and will play a more significant role in the future. One reason is that resellers have lower transaction costs. Handling products from several manufacturers, they can spread their selling costs over more products and thus make more effective use of sales calls.

CONSIDERATIONS

The soaring cost of sales calls and total selling expense become important considerations vis-a-vis the management of channels. In those companies that consider distributors to be an extension of their own sales force, the question of compensation is paramount. There may be conflict between the sales office and the distributor over who handles certain orders. If some customers are turned over to distributors, sales offices may thereafter ignore those customers, contrary to the intent of central sales management. To correct this and ensure that sales offices cooperate with distributors, companies sometimes give their salespeople incentive credit for distributor orders in their areas. This may amount to doubling credit on some orders. It raises the question of whether this is truly an incentive or merely a method of pacifying an existing sales force.

Knowing the chief advantages and disadvantages of these various channels allows producers to make better judgments concerning the path to follow and when to change course. Some considerations include status of the product life cycle, selling costs, concentration of customers, and traditions in the market. These are all subject to change over time and therefore require continual review. Unfortunately, many companies consider their distribution channels permanent and thus miss opportunities engendered by a dynamic marketing mix.

Cost Factors

As mentioned earlier, a chief consideration in evaluating channels is the control and reduction of costs. Companies who review the location and geographic concentration of customers find that certain areas are difficult to justify as direct sales territories. There is simply not enough business there to account for a fixed cost office. Others find that distributors serve many smaller customers more cost effectively. Conversely, in areas of high potential, companies may justify their own sales forces, often at lower cost. Obviously this type of decision requires market potential information as well as the relative cost of serving that market with the alternative forms of distribution.

Multiple Channels

The use of multiple channels is quite common in the business market. Companies often use their direct sales forces in high potential areas selling more complex products. In less concentrated areas, they may use reps who can justify their existence by handling several product lines. For covering smaller accounts, distributors can fill the niche, selling wide varieties of specialized items almost like a supply warehouse. The decision, therefore, is not between direct and indirect, but what meets the needs and customs of the buyers.

Unfortunately, some companies make channel decisions hastily, and therefore create unnecessary conflict within and between channels. Some conflict is expected: the trick is how to manage it well. The entire distribution system should be reviewed to ensure the highest benefit from the available alternatives. Adding incrementally to an existing strategy may only add to the problems. The review should identify the required tasks and then use the available tools to resolve those tasks. A firm should expect a channel to generate demand, arrange for physical distribution and delivery, and provide post-sale services such as routine rebuys, field service, and repair.

SHIFT FROM INDIRECT TO DIRECT

With an eye toward selling cost reduction, some firms move quickly to replace indirect channels with their own sales offices. This should be done following careful analysis of the many factors involved. It means hiring and training salespeople—a costly and time consuming process. Finding good people who are experienced enough to take over territories challenges any sales management. Establishing contact and relationships with customers previously handled by others is a whole project in itself. It means establishing a corporate presence in a new area. This can be even more difficult if the separation from the indirect channels is hostile and they remain as competitors.

Another consideration is the definition of order responsibility. If booking an order quoted three months earlier, does the intermediary get a commission or has it become a direct order? Another problem may involve changing the legal billing organization. In some cases, the producer may essentially buy out a rep, hiring all employees and absorbing their order commitments. It may mean changing the orders in the backlog (with the customer's permission) from the old to the new sales company. These are considerations to be weighed before rushing into a change that may turn out to be less desirable than anticipated.

SHIFT FROM DIRECT TO INDIRECT

This process often is the result of expansion as opposed to a reversal in marketing philosophy. There are times when a firm finds it lacks the potential to justify its own office (see Chapter 9 on marketing costs). In such cases, a local rep can fill the void and probably generate whatever business may be there. This means assuring customers that the service and product will remain the same and that the intermediary will function adequately as the company's official representative.

It is more likely that a firm will go to indirect sales through the addition of distributors. This may mean turning over smaller accounts or certain products to distributors to achieve more intensive distribution. These cases usually call for another level to an existing channel.

Locating good intermediaries means finding qualified organizations— not only to handle the product but also to relate well with the producer. This sounds deceptively easy; the competition may have signed up the best intermediaries, and an inferior organization may hurt sales, profits, and image.

EVALUATION

In deciding on the channels, certain factors must be considered:

- **Customer analysis** is necessary. How the customers buy is significant. Therefore, a customer's size, decision-making process, type of order, industry, and preference all contribute to the channel decision.

- **The geographic boundaries** also require certain decisions. Areas with heavy industrial concentrations dictate one approach, while sparsely settled areas dictate another.

- **Product** is the third major category. Some firms give a product line for the entire country to rep channels while using their sales offices for other products in the same areas. This usually occurs when the reps have expertise in particular industries, allowing the producer to concentrate in others.

- **Numbers of customers.** How many customers can a salesperson handle? This depends heavily on the geographic concentration. Account reps assigned in major cities where several major customers have headquarters in a single building find it much easier to cover them than where there is wide dispersal, as in some areas in the west.

- **The level of service and inventory.** Inventory considerations depend on the product and industry. Where JIT (just-in-time) inventory policies are practiced by customers, they will expect local stock availability. They also will expect service on product failures.

- **Degree of control necessary.** Although manufacturers need control over policies, pricing, and commitment, they may not all require details on ultimate users, applications, and the like. It is valuable but perhaps not always vital.

- **Relative cost.** The absolute cost may not be relevant. The trade-off between control and cost may be more important. The manager must consider this before making channel decisions based solely on cost.

Channel Control

Control already has been mentioned. However, there should exist a written contract that spells out the agreement between the company and its sales channel. Even with a direct sales organization, there should be a written contract stating company expectations, so that all know the operating rules. The need for a written contract with an intermediary is even more pressing. This must spell out expectations, what will be supplied by each, and the rules of termination by either party. Do not leave this as a verbal agreement, sealed by a handshake.

Cost Benefits

The cost of using one type of organization versus another is relative. The usual comparisons with expense to sales ratios may not be sufficient. Firms must take care to include all relevant costs, including support from the home office, training, and selling expenses. Comparing costs of selling through one channel versus another is more difficult than it would appear. Variations in product lines, prices, and type of customers make it difficult for accounting records to reflect cost differences. Thus there is a need to consider customer coverage, in addition to cost, in making channel decisions.

Effectiveness

The effectiveness of one channel as compared with another is heavily dependent on the people involved. Personnel with poor relational or product skills will adversely affect the results in either a direct or indirect sales organization. The type of product (simple or complex) and its position in the life cycle will affect the results. Some companies introduce change gradually. Since it can be difficult to change channels due to company philosophy or the reluctance of the sales organizations to shift gears, care is necessary to preserve morale. The sales organization must see change as an opportunity, rather than a threat.

Although permanence is often comfortable, it may not necessarily offer the best solution for handling distribution channels. Distribution often is considered the most difficult of the controllables to change (product, price, promotion, and distribution). Still, just because changes can be difficult does not mean that an outmoded or ineffective organization should be continued. Channels should be reviewed, alternatives studied, and changes instituted as conditions change within the company, product, or market.

Encourage Channel Cooperation

It's good policy to maintain cordial relations among channel members. Channel conflict often occurs because of unclear definitions of responsibility as to product or territory. Some companies go to great lengths to help their intermediaries become better businessmen. Sometimes producers run seminars on selling or accounting, specifically for intermediaries. This helps the latter in their operations and also helps cement good relationships between producer and intermediary. Intermediaries often complain of being treated like outsiders. Companies that treat intermediaries as part of the family, sharing information, training, and other kinds of help, can generate loyalty that benefits both parties. This takes more than a policy statement. It involves a philosophy that should permeate the company, including sales, engineering, manufacturing, and accounting. Once this philosophy is absorbed, a request from a rep receives the same treatment and attention as a call from a company sales office.

SUMMARY

As the part of the marketing mix that is most difficult to change, channel management requires almost constant attention. However, the difficulty in changing should not mean that once established, channels must be permanent. The foregoing illustrates that changes are not only possible but often necessary to meet the changing needs of the company.

Manufacturers have several choices in selecting channels, as shown in Figure 4-1. The evidence suggests that companies have been reviewing their alternatives and have moved in the direction of making the most of cost versus control versus customer coverage. The lowest cost may minimize control and result in unsatisfactory coverage. The highest level of control probably will mean the highest cost and the effectiveness of customer coverage may be questionable. The solution, then, is to consider all three, and mix and match to meet the specific needs of the company.

Direct channels carry the highest cost and provide the highest control. For highly complex products, with high price and long delivery, this well may be the best option. Customers may demand to deal with the producer or its direct employees, since large sums and critical performance are at stake. Further, financial circumstances may dictate direct contact between customer and producer.

Manufacturers' representatives are an essential element of channel activity. Properly trained and motivated, they can function like company account reps. Since they represent several manufacturers with complementary products, they can handle relatively complete lines. As local businesses, they often can boast customer loyalty within their areas, and they provide a vehicle for customer selling in areas that may not support the higher cost, direct sales office.

Distributors tend to handle smaller products, smaller orders, or specialized lines. As sources of local stock, they provide customers a service not always available from manufacturers. They broaden the customer base that reps and direct sales offices cannot afford to handle, selling costs being what they are.

Combinations of the above three channel components appear to offer the best solution to most channel strategies. An analysis of customers' needs and preferences and the manufacturer's preferences will lead to better decisions than merely adding to an existing force. Unfortunately, channel changes require considerable study and time, and, thus, often lead to quick fixes.

Direct sales forces that have matured in such an atmosphere often question the advisability, cost, and effectiveness of intermediaries. As such, they may not cooperate in the manner that management expects. As a prime source of channel conflict, this is a common, though not necessarily crippling situation. Most companies with multiple channels experience this situation. The challenge for sales management is to manage it while gaining control of costs, channel control, and good customer coverage.

5

Forecasting

Because of the many forecasting approaches, this topic deserves careful consideration. Although most individuals continually estimate their likely personal future, many often question the reliability of company sales forecasts. This chapter provides the following:

- The definition of a sales forecast versus other forecasts;

- Ample reasons for the necessity to forecast;

- The inherent problems associated with forecasts;

- Advantages and disadvantages of common forecast methods;

- Types of fluctuations in economic order patterns;

- Suggested method of preparing a forecast; and

- Data sources for constructing a sales forecast.

The term "forecasting" conjures up many definitions. There are forecasts of the economy, forecasts of weather, forecasts of industry movements, of company shipments and profits, of financial performance, and, yes, of new orders. Although the marketing organization may be interested in most of these, its primary concern has to do with the new order level. It is at this level that most **company** forecasts begin. Therefore, this chapter devotes itself to coverage of the individual company forecast—why and how they're done—and the caution that must be taken.

A company sales forecast as defined by Pride & Ferrell is:

> "... the amount of a product that the company actually expects to sell during a specific period at a specified level of marketing activities."[1]

Forecasting is a demanding but necessary element of a firm's comprehensive marketing program. Despite the distressing percentage of bad forecasts littering the marketing landscape, forecasting is as necessary as breathing. Although almost universally accepted, there are still skeptics.

REASONS TO FORECAST

Following are some benefits of company forecasting:

- Reduces the area of avoidable risk;
- Aids budget preparation;
- Acts as a stabilizing influence;
- Encourages employee security;
- Controls inventory;
- Backs capital requirements; and
- Promotes pricing goals.

Reduces the Area of Avoidable Risk

Forecasting by its very nature cannot be 100 percent accurate, and good management understands this. Competent forecasters do not claim they have all the answers. Forecasting is an art, not a science. Despite the many mathematical models and computerized approaches available today, many imponderables still exist. But without forecasts, business judgments are fraught with risk. There are too many unknowns even in the near term to gamble with guesses or seat-of-the-pants judgments.

Aids Budget Preparation

The development of standard costs and the preparation of operating budgets depend upon an assumed level of sales and manufacturing. To estimate expenditures and profits, one must first resolve new order levels. They are the foundations of sound profit planning.

Acts as a Stabilizing Influence

Cyclical or seasonal bumps in production and employment are costly and make business planning difficult. Premium pay rates for overtime in a temporarily overloaded plant may send costs up sharply. It is important to understand that peaks and valleys in manufacturing activity and employment levels can be minimized by good forecasts. Otherwise, remedial action hastily formed on the basis of a current demand situation can create much waste. As a stabilizing device in the hands of a purchasing department, a good forecast is extremely important, especially in these days of just-in-time (JIT) buying and scheduling. (Just-in-time refers to the inventory process where materials are not scheduled for receipt until they are needed—or just in time for production.)

Encourages Employment Security

This application relates to stabilization because of the importance of both employment and production stability. Hasty hiring and firing in response to short bursts in demand can be expensive and distracting, especially when these practices create a need to train new employees. On the other hand, a good forecast can foreshadow a deep and protracted slump in orders, a situation that may dictate a prompt reduction in personnel. This use of good business judgment can mean a considerable money saving.

Controls Inventory

Inventory control is not just a convenience; it is a necessity. In fact, some swings in the economy are characterized as "inventory corrections." If a company has built up too much inventory, it may defer stock purchases until the stock drops to more acceptable levels. When this happens across the economy, there is a national slump in buying, and the business level declines. Heavy buying of inventory at either the beginning or toward the end of an economic cycle introduces an artificial force, which, when identifiable, changes the basis of business decisions.

Backs Capital Requirements

Planning construction programs and capital requirements are especially important in those industries where the costs of plants and equipment are high. For example, it is customary for large public utilities and industrial concerns to plan years ahead. Utilities' plans must be based on power needs identified far in advance to accommodate long construction lead times. Utilities, as customers of many industrial firms, must commit to their output. This commitment creates a "derived demand" for the companies selling to the utilities. It would be difficult for any company to estimate its cash flow without a forecast of its need for capital items.

Promotes Pricing Goals

A variety of targets influence pricing, e.g., return on investment, percent return on sales, increased market share, and competitiveness. Realizing these targets cannot be accomplished after the fact. Achievement of these goals must be based on some estimate of future business levels.

RECOGNIZE THE PROBLEMS

Despite the necessity to forecast, there are many conditions that can upset predictions. Some may be anticipated, but only in general terms. Some are simply unforeseen. Following are examples of these uncontrollable variables:

1. **Competition.** Although companies know and recognize the existence of specific competitors, it is difficult to anticipate their activities. It is difficult enough to forecast one's own future. Chapter 3 covers the need and difficulty of competitive analysis.

2. **Acquisitions.** Good customers can be acquired by other companies, destroying past relationships and even cancelling existing order commitments. Another type of acquisition could involve competitors. If a larger company took over a present competitor, the merger could infuse new life

and additional money into the operation, making that competitor more formidable.

3. Customers. Situations arise where a customer goes out of business, restructures, or merely changes management, thereby altering its entire attitude toward one's own company. This may come after years of building confidence and rapport and after investing one's own time and effort toward a major project. Such changes can occur overnight, thus cancelling out a "sure thing" order.

4. Sudden economic changes. The stock market crash of 1987 was unforeseen not only by the general business community but also by the financial people. The immediate result was caution and, in many cases, deferment of major projects and commitments. As time passed, the true effect on industrial business softened, but it did cause enough disruption to delay purchases and thus invalidate order forecasts in some companies.

5. Internal conditions. Delays in shipments may generate rumors in the industry that the company cannot perform. Poor performance of a new product may create the same effect. Such information floating around among customers (and often fostered by competitors) results in a low customer confidence level that can be reflected in a lower order level. Counteracting such impressions takes some time and affects the results of the forecast.

6. Technology. Acceptance of ever-improving technology is almost a way of life. In recent years, the pocket calculator grew in popularity while its price declined sharply. The personal computer followed, with its clones and seemingly infinite software. In less than a generation, the trusty slide rule has become a relic. Proof of this constant change in state-of-the-art technology lies in the number of developments announced daily as less efficient producers go out of business or are acquired.

7. Weather. In this hi-tech age, adverse weather still can cause disruptions in business—and in well conceived forecasts. Floods, snowstorms, and drought regularly cause plant closings or worse—destruction of facilities. The effects on forecasts are obvious.

8. Politics. The political party in power of the U.S. government influences the political climate. Whether the administration is strict in enforcing laws that govern business activities becomes an important factor. Attitudes toward acquisitions, price fixing, or the like indicate the current rules of the game or at least how the rules will be enforced. This becomes part of the business climate that changes with the presidential administration's policy.

9. Budgetary control. Since the forecast often controls allowable expenses, it is possible to bias the forecast upward to gain more budget money. However, if the pressure from the top is for a higher forecast, it may provide marketing and sales departments with a basis for increased spending to fulfill those results. Thus, order forecasts relate closely to sales expense budgets.

FORECASTING METHODS

With need and related factors established, it is appropriate to review the more popular techniques used to forecast company sales. While these theories are not new, the means of fulfilling them have changed, mostly because of computers. As far back as 1947, The Conference Board, in a publication entitled *Forecasting Sales,* identified many of these techniques.[2]

1. Jury method: This approach brings together knowledgeable management personnel from within the company (e.g., sales, financial, manufacturing, engineering) to discuss the business outlook. Each manager is familiar with the company and its needs, and each brings a specialized outlook to the table. Therefore, the forecast can be done rapidly. While the foregoing is true, it still may be difficult to get a detailed forecast by product from the jury. To some extent, the results may be an expression of the vested interests of the individual members. Further, the opinions of the senior members might well prevail in such a political climate.

2. Sales force estimate: This is a popular and logical approach to sales forecasting. It works from the bottom up, using the estimates of the field sales force to arrive at a company total. This procedure can take many forms and be quite detailed. The underlying philosophy is that the salespeople are closest to the market, can provide qualitative input, and can include details by product and by customer, as required. However, one should recognize that salespeople may be more optimistic than objective. If achieving forecast determines quotas or incentives, there may be some distortion on the low side.

3. Cross-cut analysis: This method, though not as highly publicized as a formal approach, really is part of the mental process in almost any forecast. Essentially it considers the positive versus the negative factors or events that might occur in the forecast cycle. One might practice it by using two columns, one listing positive, the other negative factors. It does highlight favorable and unfavorable factors, but not being quantitative, it may not call the turning points in the cycles.

4. Customer surveys: This relates to the sales force estimate described above. Essentially, it surveys major customers for relevant data, specific or general. The field sales force, market research, or others in the organization may implement this technique. Most customers do not publicize their forecasts, since they include proprietary information. However, where salespeople have good rapport, customers may share their insights.

5. Published forecasts: In this classification, the author includes the use of outside consultants and therefore any forecast published by an outside organization. It may be subdivided into two categories: widely publicized reports by economists or research organizations; and reports that are available for a fee. A major advantage is that a specialized organization is supplying the input. However, if the procedure relies only on published material, the results are likely to be general.

6. Correlation analysis: This mathematical technique attempts to establish a relationship between the company's own sales data and a general business index or indicator. Figure 5-1 exemplifies how a company's orders may track with a national series. Note that each rises and falls in the same months of the year, and the trends are similar. With such a relationship, a movement of the indicator could signal a similar movement in the company data. It is important to remember that **correlation** does not mean **causation.** The relationship may be spurious, and although similar in direction, there could be no reason to relate them.

This method encourages the search for a lead-lag relationship, where the company sales lag the national index by a some period. Figure 5-2 displays an example of how the series would appear if the national series led the company's sales by one month. The expectation here is that movements of the national index will presage movements of the company's sales. The benefits of high correlation with a published index are obvious. One danger is the assumption that the same relationships will continue, which is not necessarily true. This, then, will distort the future values in the forecast.

7. Cycle analysis: Business cycles do exist. However, the amplitude (height) and length are not always regular. There are those who believe in fifty-year cycles. Some, subscribing to a four-year cycle, always plan a trough in any five-year forecast. The Department of Commerce publishes statistics on the leading, coincident, and lagging indicators based on cycles or, more properly, on combinations of series that tend to move cyclically. Even this complex, highly publicized set of data often emits false signals. If there were regular cycles of a consistent time span, forecasting for most companies would be simpler. Cycles should be watched as an input but not relied upon to the exclusion of other information.

8. Economic models: The computer age greatly facilitated the building of statistical models of the economy. If the principal variables that affect

Figure 5-1 National Versus Company Orders—Coincident

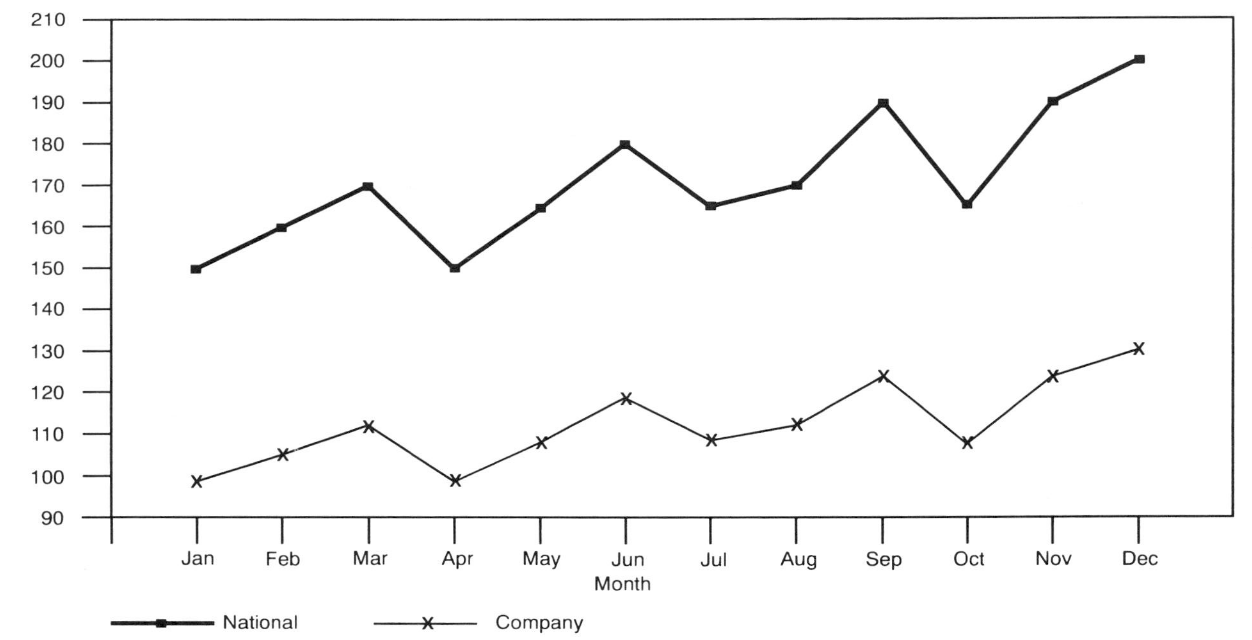

Figure 5-2 National Versus Company Orders—National Leading

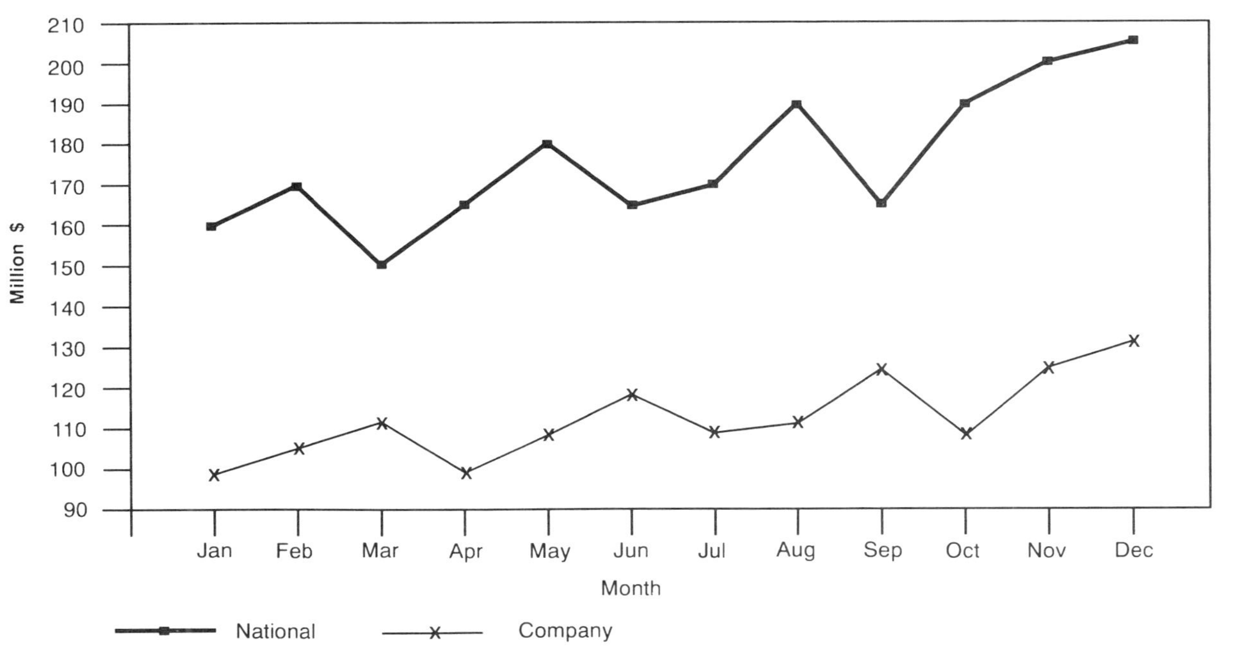

the economy can be combined in formulas so that the effect of these variables can be isolated, the practice of "what if" becomes almost instantaneous. Recognize that in some models there is the assumption that interrelationships among the data will follow tradition. This is not necessarily so, due to shifts in world power, technology, politics, social changes, and like factors. In other words, the interrelationships in the data in the future might be quite different than in the past.

9. Market tests: Industrial marketers use these tests to get customer reaction to new products. For a new product in the test phase, the company will supply a good customer with a product for evaluation in an application that exceeds a simulation. This provides on-site proof of its acceptance and performance. Such tests tell much more about a product's acceptability than a controlled laboratory test.

Some companies find it desirable to make more than one forecast. Forecast B may be truly expected and achievable. However, it is possible in rapidly changing times that business will be more favorable. In this case, invoking Forecast A provides for more optimistic performance. The lesser scenario, Forecast C, provides a fall-back position in case the economy is not as favorable as hoped. Merging the three allows for consideration of various personnel and expense levels at one time, obviating the need to repeat the entire process later in the year.

APPLICATIONS

Sales forecasts are time-specific and should cover a definite span. It is not enough to estimate that sales will increase 10 percent at some time in the future. It is necessary to forecast performance for a quarter, year, or any other period of company operations.

Company forecast cycles vary in length. As mentioned previously, since public utilities must forecast demand, their commitments and construction forecasts might extend for as long as twenty-five years. Also, they must have the ability to forecast their demand for the next peak load, which may be only a week ahead. Most other industrial-type customers fall somewhere between. It is typical for a short-range forecast to cover the coming year. A medium-range forecast covers one to five years, and a long-range forecast could extend for up to twenty-five years. Obviously, the longer the range, the more questionable the output. Long-range forecasts are based on what we know now or can theorize about the future, based on present wisdom. A look back confirms our imperfect wisdom by the unforeseen developments and progress of even the past ten years.

There should be a constant rolling check on the assumptions in the forecast and a check on actual performance against forecast. Many companies use a five-quarter update so they can look around the corner into the next year. This provides a check on actual events and provides an up-to-date look at the near term. There is nothing magic about the quarterly update. Some companies look at even shorter terms, into the weeks or months ahead. This is especially important if the business climate is soft and companies concerned with performance want to know what to do about it.

ECONOMIC FLUCTUATIONS

There are four basic types of fluctuation in the economy and therefore in a company's booking pattern.

1. **Trends** are movements over long periods, which may show gradual increases or declines in orders. Even with a flat order pattern, the effect of price increases will produce a rising long-term trend. Many companies deflate their order values for price or currency changes to reflect real growth.

2. **Cycles** are evident in the movement of national series such as gross national product. Similar movements are evident in many industries. Individual company movements may display more irregular patterns, depending on other influences.

3. **Seasonal** variations are typical in industrial orders. These may reflect customer vacation plant closings, budget cycles, or inventory cycles. Forecasting these variations can be very important to cash flow, temporary hiring, or other periodic circumstances. A new product introduced in the third quarter usually would mean overriding a normal fourth-quarter dip insofar as the firm had anticipated prompt customer acceptance.

    Knowing their seasonal patterns, some companies still forecast on a straight line basis, usually because of ease of computation. Using this technique makes performance versus forecast look favorable. If the last part of the year looks most favorable, a level forecast will show the firm to be operating above forecast for most of the year. If the rise in the last months does not materialize, the marketing manager looks bad for only a short time. This philosophy may cause many problems in other parts of the company that depend on seasonality for their planning.

4. **Random fluctuations** are caused by erratic, nonrecurring events. These unplanned, unforeseen occurrences are difficult to acknowledge in forecasting orders.

SUGGESTED APPROACHES

Check with the sales force. As those closest to the customers, salespeople's qualitative and quantitative input is essential. Whether they are direct (employees of the company) or indirect (distributors or reps), their primary data should be sought. When requesting their input, consider the following:

- Provide guidelines based on what the company plans to do to improve business: new products, better deliveries, management support, aggressive pricing, budget levels, etc.

- Supply a history of their orders by product and customer for the past five years. This puts their performance in focus and helps estimate the future.

- Request order levels by individual customer and by broad product lines. This is guessing, but who better to do it?

- Field sales managers should review individual estimates, making changes where necessary.

Request goals from corporate management for the cycle. Sometimes managers have defined in their minds the expected level of orders. If this level is not transmitted to the field and the field comes in with lower estimates, the process may require repeating. Worse yet, the field may get the impression that it is being second-guessed and that its original work represented a wasted effort.

THE PROCESS

To complete all the steps in the forecast, there should be a logical progression:

- The first request to the field should precede the fiscal year by about four months. This may sound like a long time, but each step requires time and consultation. Once the historical order material goes to the field, salespeople must make appointments with customers to discuss the coming year. Since not all customers will supply their purchasing plans, estimates must be based on the sales force's daily knowledge of customer operations. Even customers who cooperate cannot guarantee their estimates.

- When all salespeople have contacted their customers, they must get approval from their managers. The individual forecasts must then be combined into a branch or industry total for submission to the home office. At this point, comparing the new estimates with historical performance shows differences. If business is down or there are fewer salespeople, one might expect a lower estimate. However, if business is up and the company growing, one would expect this growth to show in the individual forecasts. This is a benefit of providing historical performance for comparison. Obviously this process takes weeks to fulfill.

- The home office should scan the materials as received, for logic and believability. It is not unusual for strange results to appear. As mentioned earlier, incentive pay based on forecasts may cause some salespeople to "lowball" the forecast to allow a lower quota, creating easily achievable incentives.

- While the field estimates have been progressing, home office marketing people also should be developing a parallel forecast based on product or industry department knowledge and plans. Marketing research, product planning, and strategic marketing groups should be compiling information based on the level of the economy, management input, manufacturing capacity and the like. They, too, should have had access to management guidelines regarding their expectations for the coming cycle.

  Notice here that most of the basic methods of forecasting are in play. The field sales force is using market tests and customer estimates; the home office is using various mathematical approaches, output from the executive jury, and the benefits of published data. All are important, with the forecast based on several techniques.

♦ The next step involves the reconciliation of estimates. This should be done by the cognizant managers. Field managers should meet at headquarters with product or industry managers to discuss the qualitative material behind the forecast numbers. This is not a routine approval meeting. Since each has approached the problem from a different perspective, disparities are likely, and probably will lead to trade-offs and adjustments to the original data as each brings his or her expertise to bear. A detailed review is necessary if the totals do not match the goals of management. However, since each forecast has a bias by customer, there can be logic to individual adjustments, rather than general across-the-board increases or decreases.

APPROVAL REVIEW

This new order forecast, once approved, becomes the basis for the financial profit forecast. The accounting people must translate the orders to shipments and then to profit. Throughout the process, manufacturing capacity must be considered. Overloading one facility while another stands nearly empty can compromise corporate goals. Again, any review can be conducted logically, since the necessary detail is available.

ACCURACY AND LOGIC

A check on the accuracy of prior forecasts provides a measure of confidence (or frustration) in the techniques and data used. Particularly in the personal evaluation type of format (jury, sales force), there may be a consistent, optimistic bias. Conversely, variations may swing widely over or under forecast. The example shown in Table 5-1 offers one way to check on past accuracy. The first column contains successive forecast dates during the year. The columns across the page contain the quarterly estimates, compared against the actuals at the top of the page. This yields a "batting average" of performance. This helps highlight optimism that never can foresee a decline, even in quarters that are subject to seasonal variations. Hopefully, it also will temper, not dampen, enthusiasm in future forecasts.

Table 5-1   Forecast Comparisons

	1989				1990		
Period	Qtr 1	Qtr 2	Qtr 3	Qtr 4	Qtr 1	Qtr 2	Qtr 3
Actuals	$1,000	$ 950	$1,050	$1,025	$1,050	$1,100	$1,200
Forecasts							
Jan. '89	1,000	1,000	1,025	1,000			
Mar. '89		980	1,000	950	1,100		
Jun. '89			1,040	1,000	1,050	1,050	
Sep. '89				1,050	1,110	1,110	1,300

A few words about Table 5-1: For Quarter 4 of 1989, there were four successive forecasts, in January, March, June, and September of that year. The actual turned out higher than the first three and slightly below the fourth. The September 1989 forecast was overly optimistic, each quarter achieving less than originally forecast.

Figure 5-3 illustrates how cumulative monthly data are compared with the cumulative forecast. This chart also shows the individual month in bar form, thus reflecting the monthly variations.

DATA SOURCES

What are good data sources for constructing a forecast? They can be divided into internal and external.

1. Clearly, the first source should be the **internal** sources already available within the company. All manner of order information should be accessible from sales or accounting files, or from the computer database. This material may have to be rearranged to fit the selected techniques, but once completed, it represents a rich history of actual orders. Do not neglect information that may reside in engineering and manufacturing departments.

2. The federal government provides excellent **external** information. The Commerce Department regularly publishes (some monthly) data on

Figure 5-3 Orders Versus Forecast

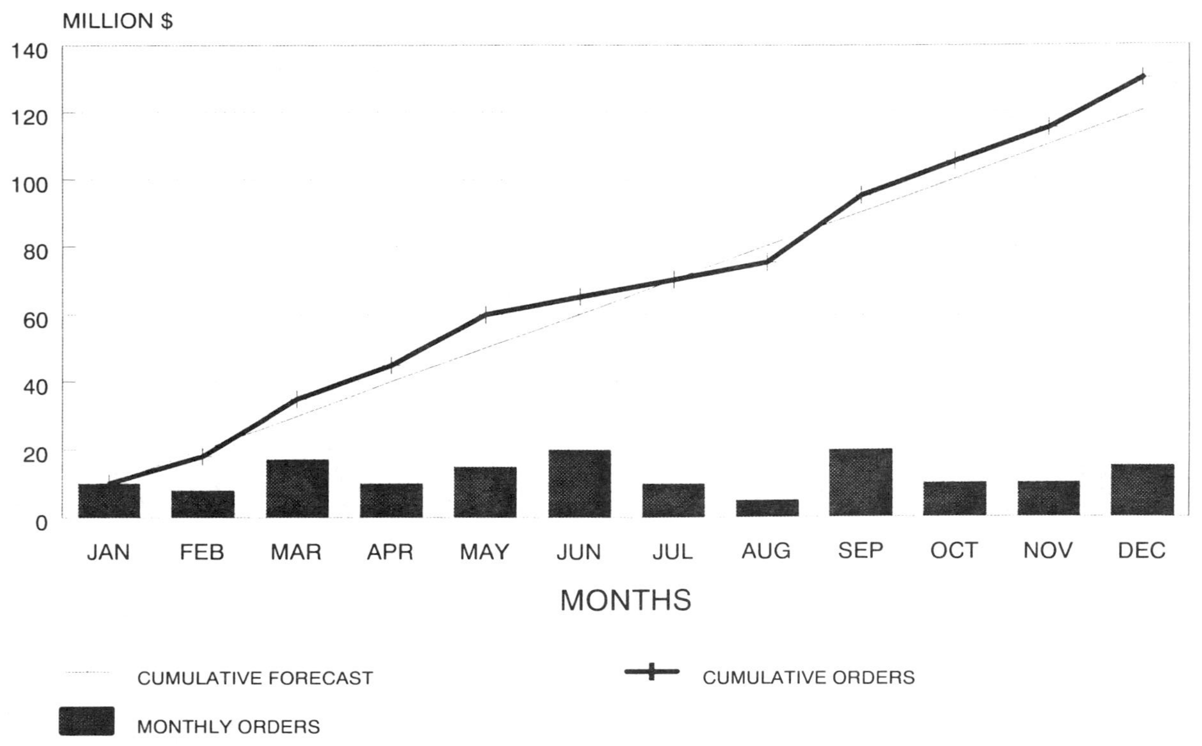

almost all segments of the U.S. economy. This provides for use of the mathematical comparison techniques and can explain aberrations that occur in the data.

For the analyst looking for mathematical techniques, there are computer programs available, with newer ones published regularly. Moreover, the *Readers' Guide to Periodical Literature* provides references on techniques that easily function on one's own computer.

Certain financial service organizations such as Dun & Bradstreet maintain established market information divisions featuring large data banks where extracted information can be tailored to one's own specifications. Such services also are available from some publishing houses. Industrial magazines often make surveys—specifically tailored to their industries or products—that contain a wealth of helpful information. Business organizations periodically publish lists of available market or forecasting references. With so much data available, it may be difficult to choose the appropriate material. Thus it is essential for the forecaster to review the company, its industries, and its history to build a qualitative and quantitative background. It is not enough to follow a forecast formula blindly. It is also necessary to have a feel for its usefulness.

SUMMARY

Forecasting is essential. Given the task, some analysts might question the needs, approaches, and sources of information. This chapter demonstrates that there is no mystery to the operation. That does not mean that it is easy. Knowing which of the benefits you seek to gain and how detailed your answer must be are two important considerations.

All forecasters must recognize the problems that are inherent in the process. The external and internal factors that influence the outcome are many. Probably the worst scenario is to assume the future will follow the path of the recent past. This chapter enumerated many important problems for consideration. This is a beginning. Be aware of them—they may lead to others that are specific to your conditions.

Forecasters add individuality to their projections. Each brings to the discipline some measure of experience and theory. Company procedures may dictate the method in the long run. All forecasters should know the level of accuracy of their company's process and continually look for better approaches. Installing a new method may be difficult where tradition is strong on a particular process.

Many computer techniques are available to those interested. This does not mean that all forecast methods are frightening. For many years, most companies made forecasts with slide rules and calculators. Today the computer has made the task simpler and faster.

Data sources are legion. Internal information is already available. Know where to look and how to get it. External sources should start with a search of government sources. These are comprehensive and inexpensive. They may not always be as timely and precise as desired, but if you are going to live in this climate, you must endure the weather.

A suggestion: use more than one method. Check one method against another. Does the output look reasonable? If not, go back and review. When the cycle is complete, review the accuracy of the original forecast. Checking several cycles may improve your accuracy by eliminating biases.

REFERENCES

1. Pride, William M., and Ferrell, O.C., *Marketing: Basic Concepts and Strategies*, 7th ed., Boston, MA: Houghton Mifflin Co., 1991, p. 127. Used with permission.
2. *Forecasting Sales*, New York, NY: The Conference Board, 1947, p. 3.

6

Call Reporting

To achieve the goal of booking new orders, controls are necessary. One important control involves sales call planning. There are many customers to visit, some friendly and others not so friendly. It requires discipline by the salesperson and the sales manager to ensure balanced coverage. This chapter describes:

- The definition of a sales call, often misinterpreted;
- The need for a call reporting program;
- The advantages and disadvantages of a formal call reporting system;
- The limited time available for calls on customers;
- The principal types of call reports: qualitative, quantitative, and mixed;
- The importance of the cost of each sales call;
- The problems associated with maintaining a call reporting system; and
- A suggested action plan for creating a call reporting program.

Is your sales call reporting system working? Are you losing orders because of a poor or inefficient reporting system? Do you care what your sales force is doing? What do you really want to know about your sales activities? Or, do you really need such a system?

DEFINITION OF SALES CALL

A sales call is a "face-to-face, personal visit with a customer." A single company may have several "customers," e.g., purchasing, engineering, manufacturing, and management. Each of these may require separate contacts or calls, with different approaches. Sales calls, in this context, do not include telephone calls or correspondence to the customer.

DETERMINATION OF NEED

The need for a call reporting system depends on the kind of information required for the orderly administration of a sales organization. This chapter addresses that issue and provides techniques and caveats associated with the creation and maintenance of an effective call report system. The needs listed below are almost self-evident. One or more of the following factors apply:

- ♦ Sales management control;

- ♦ Guidance and direction;

- ♦ Information;

- ♦ Allocation of personnel;

- ♦ Personal work plans; and

- ♦ Control of selling expense.

Sales Management Control

One of the four pillars of management is control (the other three being organizing, planning, and directing).[1] Control in this sense means adherence to the rules, not oppression. When a company is out of control, it is inefficient. It loses customers and profits, and may ultimately fail. Despite the negative connotation of the terminology, control of the sales organization through regular reporting is essential.

Guidance and Direction

The regular guidance by local and national sales managers requires information on sales activities, customer visits, and individuals' performance. With that information, sales managers can assign directions and goals to their people. Call reports facilitate this activity.

Information

Current information about customers and their purchasing plans is essential. It is also necessary to maintain good rapport as the preferred supplier. Fostering and maintaining such relationships require continual information feedback. Further, changing conditions in the industry or customer organization require adjustments in the supplier's sales tactics or strategies. Sales call reports provide this information, currently and fully.

Allocation of Personnel

Assigning sales personnel to various locations or to specific accounts must be based on the need to service customers. Industrial markets are concentrated geographically. Assignment by region and by industry is essential for proper sales coverage. Data to assist in these assignments can come from call reports.

Personal Work Plans

Sales management often fails to emphasize the benefits to salespeople of call reports. Hal Fahner highlights this in the November 12, 1984 article, "Call Reports That Tell It All" in *Sales & Marketing Management*.[2] In the article, he suggested that call reports provide salespeople with their various prospect lists. In other words, although they may not realize it, the sales force depends on call reports and literally could not function without them. This is an important selling point when introducing a call report program.

Control of Selling Expense

Today, considerable effort goes into minimizing selling cost while maximizing selling effort. Calling on customers is a major item of this cost, and it must be controlled.

ADVANTAGES OF A CALL REPORTING SYSTEM

The above needs should be convincing enough. For the managers still in doubt, the following advantages should solidify the decision:

Continuity of Information

A history on every customer is necessary. Call reports provide a running history of visits, customer personnel, major projects and the like. This is valuable proprietary information. It must be maintained even with transfers of salespeople. It would be a major loss if a salesperson left the supplier company with the only record of major customers.

Maintenance of Marketing Database

Many, if not most, industrial companies now maintain a marketing information system. Such a system contains information on products, salespeople, industry, and, importantly, on individual customers. This information is used in forecasting, competitor analyses, sales planning, etc. Call reports are prime data sources for such systems.

Customer Relationships

A study of sales calls can be a valuable source of information on the supplier's relationship with the customer. Qualitative comments in the reports provide a running commentary. An inadequate number of calls on a major account signals a different condition. Intensive knowledge of a customer's plans provides a strategy base for the supplier.

Expense Control

Call reports provide a check on travel expenses. High travel expenses look suspicious when all sales calls are local. One company noted that on the week preceding Christmas, several salespeople limited their calling to nearby accounts (thus allowing time for shopping). Overcalling on certain accounts is expensive and wasteful, particularly if the potential is low.

Memory Jogger

Salespeople also need memory joggers in their planning. Since customer calling must be planned in an efficient manner, call schedules must be planned and appointments arranged well in advance. Call reports are a valuable tool when creating itineraries (to be discussed later in this chapter).

Provides for Smooth Operation

A common complaint in any organization refers to the time taken "putting out fires." Planning loses out in the battle of everyday problems. A call report program requires the initial planning by the salesperson and provides an output that makes for consistent operations.

DISADVANTAGES OF CALL REPORT SYSTEMS

Like most other activities, call report programs have their detractors. There are a few common objections.

Wasted Effort

The salesperson may seldom see the results of his or her call reports. It does take time, and if no tangible result is obvious, the system is faulted. The home office also incurs cost to read, tabulate, and analyze reports. Some say this is not productive.

False or Inaccurate Reporting

Some home office personnel suspect that salespeople falsify reports to cover higher expense reporting. Since call reports often are not checked out with customers, this may be a valid complaint in certain cases.

Noncompliance

In spite of well documented rules, some sales personal repeatedly neglect to submit reports. This may be tolerated by sales managers who do not fully support such programs. If permitted, it clearly is a disadvantage. It need not be a problem if it is a part of the salesperson's evaluation.

No Significant Value

This complaint comes from home office personnel who find no beneficial data from the reports. If there is no new or important information, perhaps the report needs changing. Determine the information needed and tailor the system around that. Jack Falvey's article, "There's No Call for Call Reports," in the November 1989 *Sales & Marketing Management*, covers an alternative to call reports.[3] He suggests pre-call reports that set detailed objectives for selected projects before the call.

The need for call reports has been established. The weight of the advantages over disadvantages confirms the value. The next consideration is to proceed, which leads to a study of the system design. The marketer has the choice of three basic approaches: qualitative, quantitative, or mixed. To make this decision requires a determination of basic philosophy. The company may want better control of the sales force or more management information. It may wish to help salespeople in their personal planning or any combination of the needs listed previously.

INFORMATION REQUIRED

Considerable management information can be extracted from call reports. The data can include the following:

- ◆ Customer name and address;
- ◆ Person contacted;
- ◆ Decision-makers;
- ◆ Annual potential;
- ◆ Products discussed;
- ◆ Result of call;
- ◆ Projects outstanding;
- ◆ Date projects expected to be placed;
- ◆ Percent chance of getting order;

♦ Action to be taken; and

♦ Next planned call.

There is no single, correct list of required information. Each company must decide for itself what data it needs and how it is going to use it. This will be clearer as we proceed.

CALL QUOTAS

Before establishing a quota of calls per day for your sales force, review your company operations.

1. Are branch offices staffed with enough "inside" people to handle technical or clerical questions from customers? If so, this allows the direct salespeople to make more calls and thus increase face-to-face time with customers.

2. Do your salespeople have longevity with the company? If so, they are likely to have three or four weeks of vacation per year, thus affecting the number of available working days. With these qualifications in mind, you can provide your average number of working days.

TOTAL AVAILABLE CALL TIME

Salespeople do not work 365 days a year. Nor can they call on customers every day for eight hours a day. *Sales & Marketing Management*, in its "1991 Sales Manager's Budget Planner" (June 17, 1991) defined the number of selling days as:[4]

> "4 days x 52 weeks per year, less 6 holidays and 15 days vacation and/or sick leave, resulting in a figure of 187 days." (The assumption is that one day per week will be spent in the office.)

This is a good general average. Still, it must be tempered with product and company variations. Some companies use five days/week for fifty-two weeks less ten holidays and ten days vacation. This would result in a value of 240 days. The need for care is obvious in making comparisons.

With no inside help in a branch office, a salesperson may spend only two or three days per week in the field, creating another condition.

QUALITATIVE REPORTS

With these preliminaries settled, the qualitative approach will be discussed first. There are many possible formats. It is not unusual for companies to revise formats as their managements or needs change. Figure 6-1 displays the layout and data requirements of a typical qualitative report. (For samples of other types, see the report entitled "Salesmen's Call Reports" published by The Conference Board.[5])

Figure 6-1 is self-explanatory and does not require the salesperson to reference detailed instructions and tables for codes and data. The form itself contains sufficient instructions. Although this simple format may not appear to be a plus factor, it is a positive approach in the salesperson's eyes.

Advantages of Qualitative Reports

1. Qualitative reports allow the salespeople to describe just what happens on a call or how matters stand with the customer. This information is helpful, particularly for sales managers reviewing customer files before making field visits. With sales calls spaced weeks or even months apart, memories of the last call surely are dimmed. The brief synopsis contained in a qualitative report recalls the actual meeting and references important topics for review.

2. Qualitative remarks can reference changes in the customer organization, large new orders received, plans for expansion, or other pertinent information. These narratives should reference other reports to sales management requesting assistance or just provide feedback on key accounts. (Physicians often use qualitative files, dictating for the file the results of each patient visit immediately following the visit.)

3. Qualitative call information provides insights to persons not present at the call. Sales managers need to be informed promptly and regularly of activity with certain accounts. These managers may be in a local branch office or may be located in a home office far away. They give key accounts preferential treatment. Prompt reports on these accounts provide that feedback.

Figure 6-1

WEEKLY CALL SUMMARY

Acct Rep:________________________   Branch Office:________________________

Date	Customer Name And Location	Time Spent	Contacts	Call Summary

Disadvantages of Qualitative Reports

1. Qualitative reports make it more difficult to arrive at comparative numerical totals by salesperson. Many companies maintain records of calls per day or calls per product by individual salespersons. There may be call quotas involved by product or by account and this form makes such counting cumbersome.

2. Also, since the qualitative format involves a narrative, **salespeople often use it to obtain immediate responses to customer requests,** office needs, or the like. Such requests do not belong in call reports, nor should they be included in expense reports. They should be handled in separate correspondence to the person who can fill the request. Some companies provide special forms for this purpose to prevent such usage. Unfortunately, call reports not due for immediate processing may sit in the "in basket" of a sales manager, exacerbating this problem.

3. Incomplete or sketchy information can make a report practically useless. Thus it may have no value qualitatively or quantitatively. The documentation must impress the sales force on the need for clarity and completeness.

QUANTITATIVE REPORTS

The quantitative type of report provides sales management with the opportunity to summarize and compare salespeople and territories, despite the lack of narrative comments. In this approach, the salesperson completes a multiple-choice format, e.g., products, frequency of call, and reason for the call. This can be on a hard copy input form that is later converted into computer copy, or it can be entered directly into a computer from the field. Figure 6-2 illustrates a hard copy weekly call report form using the quantitative method.

Advantages of Quantitative Reports

1. The simple format can be completed quickly after a brief review of the layout. There is no need to compose a narrative, perhaps couched to impress superiors. The report often can be completed immediately after the call while the results are still fresh in memory.

2. Processing by the home office is rapid. Coded results provide for computer processing in many combinations; product, industry, customer,

Figure 6-2

WEEKLY CALL REPORT

Name: _________________

Office: _________________

<u>Dept. Visited</u>
P - Purchasing
E - Engineering
O - Operations
M - Maintenance
O - Other

	Customer Name and Location	Call Date	Dept Vis	Motors	Pumps	Pulleys	Controls	Boilers	Ovens
				Products Discussed					
Mon									
Tues									
Wed									
Thur									
Fri									

Instructions: Enter appropriate information for columns 2–6. (May be hand written.) Mark X in products you discussed.

quota, etc. Accordingly, the reports are ready for analysis quickly and in multiple copies, if necessary, without manual processing.

3. Feedback is provided to the salesperson, confirming that the call reports were not merely filed without review. Since this was a problem cited earlier, its correction minimizes field objections.

Disadvantages of Quantitative Reports

1. The summaries consist of hard, cold numbers. Since there is no provision for qualification of the call result, the numbers tell it all. This assumes that everything is either black or white; the call was made or not made. This may be frustrating to a salesperson trying to crack an account.

2. Repetitiveness leads to *lack of attention to detail.* Since all calls use the same format for all situations, entering results is a boring routine, appearing to be without purpose. This condition leads to laxity in completing reports or to deferring them unnecessarily.

Internal Procedures

The procedure for handling quantitative reports rests with the home office.

1. A program must be designed to handle input, process it, and provide for usable output. It should be user-friendly. The data processing details are beyond the scope of this book. Our concern is with input and output, not processing.

2. The home office processes weekly input (Figure 6-2) through a computer and issues a Monthly Call Summary Report covering the results of the present month's calls plus a history of calls for the year (Figure 6-3). This summary lists all the salesperson's customers, including those called on and those not visited. Notice the similarity between this form and the Weekly Call Report form (Figure 6-2) completed by the salesperson.

3. The computer program accumulates the year-to-date data and summarizes the references to the annual quota and number of planned calls. This, then, provides a composite list of the month and year-to-date activity with each customer. Thus it highlights the coverage **frequency** of the major accounts. However, it does not report the **quality** of the coverage. If necessary, summary reports by region or branch office may be created for management's review.

4. Include certain standardized codes in the system. Each salesperson supplies the home office with a list of customers and prospects by loca-

Figure 6-3

MONTHLY CALL SUMMARY

Name: _________________

Office: _________________

Dept. Visited	Annual Potential
P - Purchasing	1 - Not a User (Consultant, etc.)
E - Engineering	2 - $10,000 to $50,000
O - Operations	3 - $50,000 to $100,000
M - Maintenance	4 - $100,000 to $500,000
O - Other	5 - Over $500,000

Customer Name and Location	Ind	Month			Pot	Annual		Products Discussed					
		Call Date	Dept Vis	Call Quota		Call Quota	Calls Made	Motors	Pumps	Pulleys	Con-trols	Boilers	Ovens

Month		
Call Quota	Tot Calls Made	Major Calls Not Made

Tot Calls by Product This Month					
M	PM	P	C	B	O

tion. (One code is not enough for all the facilities of a diverse company such as Exxon.) This list includes (for marketing):

♦ Customer name and address;

♦ Annual potential;

♦ Annual planned call frequency;

♦ Products normally purchased; and

♦ SIC (Standard Industrial Classification).

For financial and other purposes, the customer code may include mailing address, credit rating, and other pertinent information. The home office assigns a unique code containing this information, cross-referenced to the branch office and the salesperson. This serves as the master code for calls, prospects, orders, and billings.

5. Create a table of annual relative potential. Although contained on the form, it is necessary to position it as a computer table as well. This guide highlights overcalling on small accounts with limited potential. It also shows where high potential accounts have too few calls. Table 6-1 uses a single code to identify approximate annual potential.

Table 6-1   Annual Potential Codes

1. Not a user (consultants, etc.)

2. $10,000 to $50,000

3. $50,000 to $100,000

4. $100,000 to $500,000

5. Over $500,000

A product listing similarly defines the product lines for the computerized summary:

Motors	Controls
Pumps	Boilers
Pulleys	Ovens

As previously stated, the quantitative method is more complex in that it requires salespeople to follow detailed instructions and to reference codes and tables. Once the home office has the computer program in place, the processes of totaling and reporting back to the field are routine.

Although sales forces do not greet call reports enthusiastically, sales managers should provide positive reinforcement. The advantages to the individual and to the company should be stressed.

MIXED FORMAT REPORTS

The mixed type of call report combines qualitative and quantitative features. Though there is provision for narrative, a checklist routinely handles products, applications, status, and the like. The instructions are self-explanatory, and completion of the report is simple. The Sales Report in Figure 6-4 illustrates this method. If either the qualitative or quantitative formats are too extreme, the mixed type provides a suitable compromise.

SALES CALL COSTS

Sales & Marketing Management reported that an industrial sales call cost $250.54 in 1990. The following table (Table 6-2) shows how this value has grown in recent years.[6]

If a company works on an expense-to-sales ratio of 10 percent for field operations, that would preclude calling regularly on any account with less than about $10,000 annual potential. This assumes that an account must be visited at least every three months to maintain continuing relationships.

Table 6-2   Cost Per Call

1986	$178.96
1987	207.21
1988	217.92
1989	224.87
1990	250.54

Figure 6-4

SALES CALL REPORT

Account Rep:_______________________________   Date:_____________

Branch Office:_______________________________

Assisted By:_______________________________

Customer Name & Location:____

Names & Titles of People Contacted: Products Discussed
                                                   Number in order of importance

_______________________________   Motors
                                                          Pumps
_______________________________   Pulleys
                                                          Controls
_______________________________   Boilers
                                                          Ovens

Type of Call (Check one or more):

      Cold   Inquiry
      Follow Up   Service
      Lost Order   Other

Summary of Call and Status:

____

____

____

____

____

____

Any less activity should be handled by telephone or by mail. The following mathematical calculations illustrate this thesis.

Minimum number of calls per year 4
Industry average cost per call $250.54
Desired expense-to-order ratio 10%

4 x $250.54 (per call) = $1,002.16 (total call expense)
$1,002.16 / 10% = $10,021.60 (minimum expected orders)

An account with a potential of only $5,000 would merit only about two calls per year—hardly enough for the salesperson to be remembered by the customer. Still, this is a general statement, based upon averages. Each company must calculate its own ratios and qualify its data accordingly.

There must be other rules as well for call reports.

♦ Each call requires a separate report for each department visited.

♦ Due dates for report submission must be specified.

♦ Cold calls on customers without sufficient potential should be noted. Give call credit, but do not add the account to the active customer list.

MAJOR PROJECT REPORTS

Although not truly call reports, major project reports provide similar important information on major activities planned by customers. Each month field sales managers submit lists of projects expected as orders to the home office. The managers update these lists continually as conditions change. Orders, as received, are matched against these lists, as shown in Table 6-3. Since the report shows order date, customer, product, percent chance, and shipment date, the company can maintain a running status report of important negotiations. They provide a current "hot list" of accounts needing attention. Table 6-3 is an example of a major project report.

Where this detail is not sufficient, companies compile a database of all current projects. Each account representative is responsible for keeping his projects current. These projects are sorted in different categories, such

Table 6-3   June Major Projects
Over $100K and 70% Chance   **In $1,000**

STATUS	REGION	CUSTOMER NAME	VALUE	PERCENT CHANCE	SHIP DATE
Order	West	Exxon-Baytown	500	80	Dec.
Lost	Central	Acme-Chicago	250	70	Nov.
	East	Mobil-Delaware	875	90	Dec.
Delay	West	Jones Co-Seattle	125	75	Oct.

as salesperson, industry, product, percent chance, and date of expected order. Monthly summaries may be issued to sales management. Simpler programs also can be created on personal computers with friendly software.

MANAGERS' REPORTS

Call reporting is not limited to account representatives. Many companies require branch and regional managers to complete them. General sales managers should be interested particularly in their first line of regional managers and how they service major accounts. Regional managers are senior representatives of the company and thus bear major responsibility for personally managing certain key accounts.

ITINERARY REPORTS

Call reports are related to itinerary reports. While call reports list **what has happened,** itinerary reports list **planned calls** for the week or month ahead. Additionally, they require the salesperson to plan calls, rather than make them in a haphazard, unscheduled fashion. Also, itineraries provide the sales office with a listing of locations where the salesperson may be reached. It is not uncommon for an account representative to proceed directly to a customer's office in the morning and from there travel to other cities. If it is necessary to contact him or her, the itinerary provides a schedule of time and location. Figure 6-5 illustrates a typical itinerary report.

Figure 6-5

WEEKLY ITINERARY REPORT

Name:_______________________   Week Beginning: _______________

Office:_______________________

	Location	Calls Planned	Contact
Sun.	City Hotel		
Mon.	City Hotel		
Tues.	City Hotel		
Wed.	City Hotel		
Thurs.	City Hotel		
Fri.	City Hotel		
Sat.	City Hotel		

Salespeople tend to operate as independent practitioners. In some companies, the salespeople seldom visit their branch offices, instead dealing with their offices by telephone or computer link. When a salesperson must report to the branch office before starting out on daily calls, he or she may find it necessary to cross the city or cross the territory and then double back for the first call. This is inefficient. Further, once a salesperson arrives at his branch office, routine expressions of camaraderie may delay leaving on that first call. Some companies suggest that the salesperson proceed directly to the first call and not "check in" at the office until the end of the day.

The salesperson sets the pace, decides on whom to call and what is to be said to the customer. He or she becomes the company's official representative to that customer. Little wonder that these "independent business people" reject a type of reporting that many consider unnecessary and obstructionist. As mentioned earlier, control is necessary not only at the top level but also to the level of each salesperson's contact.

Continued relationships with customers are essential in the industrial field. Call reports provide a useful history developed over the years. If the salesperson kept this information only in the "little black book" maintained by the salesperson and that person left the company with this record, a large gap would need to be bridged.

PROBLEM AREAS

Although the foregoing describes various types of call report programs, those programs are not without problems. Before designing and enforcing a new or revised system, the following should be considered:

Discipline: Most people don't like to be controlled. Salespeople often balk at the tedious work involved in filling out call reports, expense reports, major project reports, or other paperwork required by the home office. They pose the standard question, "Do you want me to sell or fill out reports?" The standard answer is, "Both."

Reports should be filled out immediately after a sales call, since the information is still fresh in mind. More likely, the salesperson will wait until the end of the week or month, whenever completed reports are due. When the salesperson takes the few minutes required to complete the report immediately, the company gains. If there is a delay in the report until the end of the week, five days and several calls have intervened. This dims the recollection of that first call of the week.

Lack of compliance: Some salespeople will avoid filling out call reports altogether. When there is no apparent use or feedback from submitted reports, salespeople question their value. Sales managers should emphasize that reporting is part of the job description and a factor in merit evaluations. The value to the individual and to the company must be highlighted.

Biased information: Depending on the type of call report used, some salespeople will include only favorable information in a report. Anything implying failure to cover the account properly, inefficient selling, or being outsold, will be omitted. Reading call reports often gives the impression that price and delivery cause most lost sales. Since the salesperson often has no control over these two factors, they are a convenient excuse. Call reports must be factual, not coverups or sounding boards for inefficiency.

ACTION PLAN

The foregoing represents an overview of the various methods of reporting calls and an assessment of certain problems. For the analyst who already has a system in operation or who wants to design a new one, the following suggests a workable process:

- Define your company needs for this information;

- Decide what you want to know and when;

- Can you get this information any other way?;

- Decide on qualitative, quantitative, or mixed format;

- If a new system, provide for field testing;

- If a revision, emphasize why changed and state benefits;

- Establish a home office person responsible for the program;

- After the system is in operation, check if it meets the original, specified needs;

- See that all persons report completely and on time;

- Provide regular feedback to the field; and

- Periodically review results and change when necessary.

Evaluation of Present System

The following discussion serves as an audit for your present system, with suggestions for improvement. As in most studies, you must determine your present relative position.

Sales & Marketing Management and *McGraw-Hill Research* are two widely publicized sources of call costs. Your trade or professional association also may collect and publish such data. However, as cautioned earlier, use this data with discretion, ensuring that your measurements are relevant. Another source of comparison is your own history. If the latter is not available, exhaust every effort to generate that background information.

Another approach involves "benchmarking," a technique described by David Altany in his article "Copycats" in *Industry Week* (November 5, 1990). In this approach, the company uses a

> "... formal process of measuring and comparing a company's operations, products, and services against those of top performers both within and outside the company's primary industry."[7]

The goal is to look outside the company to learn the secrets of success of the industry's leaders. It thus goes beyond the mentality of managers who look only to improve last year's performance.

At this point, an additional piece of information is useful. Since there are many variations even within industries, your company may not match up organizationally on a **cost per call** basis. Therefore, it is wise to calculate a **cost per day** for your sales force. Compare this with the cost per day of the published data. It may improve your analysis of the situation.

If not satisfied with your cost per call or cost per day results, consider reviewing your philosophy of doing business.

Areas Requiring Attention

1. Many companies accept the status quo. They believe their people are doing the best possible job. It is assumed that the present must be right, particularly if history bears out present performance.

2. Some sales managers, having risen through the ranks, did not believe in call reports then and do not believe in them now. This lukewarm attitude fosters noncompliance.

3. The ratio of outside people who call on customers may be disproportionate to the inside support people. If you calculate the relative cost of an inside person, you will find the cost is much lower than the cost of a direct person. It is uneconomical to use the higher-priced people for office duty.

4. The territorial layout or account assignments may require attention. As changes occur over the years, inefficiencies appear, creating travel patterns that are extremely wasteful. In addition to salespeople passing one another locally, sometimes they must travel into other territories to reach assigned accounts. Further, small, unprofitable accounts may remain in the call patterns.

5. Paperwork, always the bane of salespeople, often cuts into prime selling time. Is your required paperwork oppressive? Is it all necessary? Order entry is a function often subject to improvement. You should make it as easy as possible to enter orders from the field. Electronic order entry may solve this problem. Often touted as a significant time saver, it may in fact be burdening direct salespeople not familiar with all the requirements.

SUMMARY

In summary, call reports are a **significant element of planning** from the bottom to the top. Companies should foster planning at the account level, and reinforce the idea that it is not only for the company but also for the individual's benefit. Also, the company gains an audit trail of the coverage of major accounts and the daily performance of salespeople. Call reports may be simple or complex, qualitative, mixed, or quantitative. If the company customarily requires detailed reporting, the problem is half solved. Instituting a complex system where none previously existed probably will meet with resistance. If the system results only in a set of reports without action or feedback by sales management, it likely will deteriorate and ultimately fail. Look at your conditions carefully before deciding on the type and amount of information required.

Be careful of comparisons with published data. The data may be perfectly correct but may not match your definitions. Make sure these comparisons are valid. If obtaining good external data is difficult, compare your present data with your history to show trends.

Don't limit call information to compiling call report summaries only. Use the data for input on outstanding quotations and major projects. There is a wealth of information contained in a good system.

Major project reports constitute a powerful short-range method of forecasting large orders. Although not truly call reports, their basis is information gained from customer calls. They should be current and accurate. Experience gained in operating a major project system will fine-tune it to a major sales tool.

Despite care in the design of a call report system, there is still the necessity of administration. Compliance by all is necessary. Attention to input and use of the information are key factors. If the present system is not working, look for the reasons, and, if necessary, reconstitute the process.

The time is past for free-wheeling sales forces operating only on intuition. Top performance and measurement of that performance is essential for success—and ultimately for survival.

REFERENCES

1. Terry, George R., *Principles of Management*, 6th ed., Homewood, IL: Richard D. Irwin Inc., 1972, p. 4.
2. Fahner, Hal, "Call Reports That Tell It All," *Sales & Marketing Management*, Nov. 12, 1984, pp. 50-52.
3. Falvey, Jack, "There's No Call For Call Reports," *Sales & Marketing Management*, Nov. 1989, pp. 122-123.
4. "1991 Sales Manager's Budget Planner," *Sales & Marketing Management*, June 17, 1991, p. 6. Reprinted by permission.
5. *Salesmen's Call Reports*, New York, NY: The Conference Board, 1972, pp. 22-95.
6. "1991 Sales Manager's Budget Planner," op. cit., p. 72.
7. Altany, David, "Copycats," *Industry Week*, Nov. 5, 1990, pp. 11-18.

7

Planning

Every company must define its direction. A plan puts marketing decisions into proper perspective, sometimes highlighting the need for a change in focus. Since marketing is the first step in the planning process, it influences the corporate plan throughout. Any change in the marketing plan filters through to all functions. This chapter highlights:

- The reasons behind planning;
- Various time frames for marketing plans;
- Typical approaches: top down and bottom up;
- Suggested process in constructing a plan;
- Dependence of other functions on the marketing plan; and
- Common failings in planning.

Sound planning is an integral part of every good organization. Although the planning function is treated more formally by some companies, nearly all have at least informal goals, as well as ideas on how to achieve them. Marketing literature is replete with books and articles on planning, its history, need, methods, and pitfalls.

Planning can assume many forms. It may focus on marketing, finance, manufacturing, or others functions, all of which may contribute to a total corporate strategy. Some define strategic planning as developing and articulating the long-range objectives of a business. Operational planning covers the development of detailed programs to achieve those objectives. This chapter focuses on the marketing sector and its contribution to the total corporate plan.

In the 1970s, the problems of the business world cast doubts on the merits of planning, and there were, as a result, wholesale eliminations of planners and their departments. This has changed. It appears that good planners are held in the highest esteem as they concentrate not only on marketing activities, but on human resources and other activities that impact on total corporate objectives.

REASONS TO PLAN

Proponents of planning have used similar reasons for justifying this activity. The following list represents some typical rationales. Planning:

- Improves earnings and profits;
- Makes better use of company facilities and abilities;
- Improves stability;
- Encourages systematic forward thinking;
- Meets technological change; and
- Provides preparation for sudden developments.

These are all worthwhile concepts. Many more could be added to reinforce the function's value. Despite this, the challenges encountered in planning often hinder design of a plan. The first step may be the most difficult—where to begin. The first-time assignment of preparing a planning outline or framework is intimidating.

Accurate plan results sometimes seem completely out of reach due to so much interdependence. Many conditions are outside the control of the planner, and many things can go awry. Under these circumstances, the first plan may fall below expectations. Such factors as methods, the relative importance of certain items, and the ability to educate participants all contribute to the planning process. An initial failure should be viewed as a valuable learning experience in a complex discipline, not as a reflection of incompetence.

SPAN OF PLANS

Occasionally the terminology may be confusing. To forestall that possibility, the following terms will be used in this chapter:

- Short-range plan—up to one year;

- Medium-range plan—one to five years;

- Long-range plan—five years and longer;

- Strategic plan—company's mission, objectives, goals, business portfolio, and growth strategy; and

- Marketing plan—framework and activities to be performed by the marketing division.

Some practitioners use the terms "planning" and "forecasting" interchangeably. They do differ in that **forecasting is a component of planning.** The forecast estimates the future. The plan provides the method of achieving that forecast, with alternatives and contingencies.

APPROACHES TO PLANNING

Not all companies approach planning in the same manner. Some use a "top down" approach where management supplies a target or goal, and the staff planners create a plan designed to accomplish those objectives. Other companies use a "bottom up" approach, where the planners create the plan, present it to management for approval, then modify it to accommodate the goals of management. In either case, the chief executive is the company's chief planner, whether as the author of the original goal or the source of final approval.

If top management is not recognized as being fully behind the plan, that plan will become just another report. As time progresses and detours block the path of achievement, the questions always should be: (a) Does the plan anticipate this issue? and (b) If not, what do we have to do to accommodate this problem and still meet the plan?

As the foregoing suggests, the strategic plan of the company encompasses more than just marketing. It should cover human relations, manufacturing capacity and capability, financial considerations, management skills and depth, and other needs and strengths. However, marketing, being at the front end, provides significant input. It supplies the new order forecast and data on the climate both of the economy and the company's marketplaces. Therefore, marketing will be highlighted as the initiator of most of the input to the corporate plan.

Four major questions must be addressed in preparing a marketing plan. The simplicity of the questions may make the assignment less intimidating.

1. Where have we been?
2. Where are we now?
3. Where do we want to go?
4. How can we get there?

The applications or techniques prompted by these questions are legion. The specific needs of the available talent and facilities may dictate various approaches, but the questions are essentially the same. In this chapter, a typical business will be detailed, realizing that it is only one among many. However, no matter what the specifics of the approach, the processes will be similar. The components covered are typical and can be arranged to suit almost any company's structure.

If management's objective is "growth in sales and profit," leaving the rest to the separate divisions or business units, those managers become their own planners. Their plans are really subsets of the total corporate plan. When the division managers acknowledge their roles as planners, the plans take on more significance than if they had been formulated by a central staff group.

To move into the uncertain future with a growth goal and provision for contingencies requires a knowledge of where the division stands and how it got there. This requires answers to the first two of the above four questions. A leap into the future from an uncertain position could be dangerous and perhaps fatal.

ACTION PLAN

Despite the format used, there are certain steps that should be followed, no matter how simple or complex the final procedure:

- Define company objectives;

- Define organization, set schedules;

- Review past and present (situation analysis);

- Define action to be taken; and

- Follow up.

Define Company Objectives

These objectives must be clear to all, for planning without goals makes little sense. While long-term profitability is the apparent goal of most companies, there are many other objectives: best market share, price leader, most innovative, best known and respected, and many others. Define them and put them in sequence of their importance. This will be a measuring scale.

Define the Organization, Set Schedules

Defining the organization is a two-part step. First, look at the existing organization. Is it defined by product, industry, geography, or a combination of the three? The second step is to modify it if necessary.

1. Depending on the similarity of **products,** companies may organize by discrete product lines, such as special products for aircraft only versus pumps for general industry versus rolling mills for the steel industry. There is merit to grouping similar products. Every product has a life cycle. Ever-changing high technology products have much shorter cycles than heavy pumps, for example. Creating divisions for these similar products improves operations. These may be independent divisions with their own engineering, sales, or

manufacturing capabilities, where the division head has full profit responsibility and performs almost like a company president.

2. Some companies may organize by **industry** business unit. Here the concentration is on individual industries such as paper or petroleum, regardless of product line. This provides for expertise in product application. The business unit directors may be responsible for sales, distribution, engineering, service, or the like. Functions common to all industries such as accounting, human resources, and manufacturing would report higher up in the firm. This type of organization sells all products in all geographical areas.

3. Still other companies may operate **geographically** for sales and service, with all other activities governed as a single entity. This type of sales force sells all products to all industries. Engineering, accounting, human resources, and manufacturing exist as separate operations reporting to the company president.

4. The other major organization component involves the responsibility for **coordination** of the plan. Although the president is the chief planner, and the division or business unit heads are the operational planners, an individual or group must be designated to handle the details. Written procedures, follow-up with the participants, preparation of preliminary results, and many other details require continual attention. This person or group should report directly to the president. That gives management's stamp of approval and allows access to top levels as planning proceeds.

5. **Timeliness** is significant in planning. If there is insufficient time, the work will be hurried at the expense of accuracy and attention. If the planning cycle is too long, conditions may have changed by the time the plan is completed. In any case, produce a written schedule and follow it. Realistically, budget several months for the entire process.

Past events set the stage for analysis and suggest decisions calculated to ensure future success. Where the company is subdivided into industry or product divisions, it is good to build the plans at that level. That size element is more manageable, and the product or industry group has some consistency for analysis and projection. Requesting this information of the division managers assures their participation and accountability.

Internal Review

Before leaping off into uncharted waters by constructing a marketing plan with many variables, review your situation. There is a wealth of information in your own company. It may save you considerable external study.

Reconstruct History

It is useful to construct a ten-year history of total divisional orders and shipments. Figure 7-1 provides a suggested format. This history puts the division performance into focus—whether and when it grew and by how much. This information should be compiled by the division, since it will emphasize to that group its true growth. The entire complexion of the company and industry may have changed over this period, and this will verify at which period that occurred.

Review Details of Products and Markets

This chart should display more detailed information but need only cover the past three years. Figure 7-2 illustrates this. Note that this chart reports at the product level within the division. This precludes mixing very different products with different markets, cycles, and the like. The chart format requests information on pretax profits, the estimated available market, and the estimated percent of that market the company achieved. The size of the available market is difficult to define for individual product lines. Census figures based on shipments are late and often are too general for detailed comparisons. Trade association reports often represent only a part of the industry, and reporting may be sporadic. This highlights the need for good estimates to get from "here" to the final goal. Again, this information puts past and present performance into proper focus.

Estimate Industry Penetration

Based on historical patterns, each dominant product line should be reported and subdivided into the major purchasing industries. Figure 7-3 provides an example of format. This will establish whether the market focuses on a few industries or covers several. Since industries may reflect cyclical buying practices, a three-year average may be used.

Figure 7-1

CORPORATE PLAN

Historical Review

Division_________________   In $1,000

Year	New Orders	Shipments
1981		
1982		
1983		
1984		
1985		
1986		
1987		
1988		
1989		
1990		

Figure 7-2

CORPORATE PLAN

Historical Review

Division______________   In $1,000

Product____________

PRODUCT	**1988**	**1989**	**1990**
Orders			
Shipments			
Pretax Profit			
Available Market			
Percent Market Achieved			

Figure 7-3

CORPORATE PLAN

Historical Review

Division________________   In $1,000

Product_______________

Industry   **New Orders**

Private
Utilities

Food

Paper

Government
  Federal
  State
  Local

Textile

Petroleum

Chemical

Gas

Steel & Alum.

Automotive

Drugs

O.E.M.

Other

Competitive Information

Due to its impact on history, the analysis should include competitive information. Construct a table comparing each product with the competition's activities in such areas as price, performance, shipment, design, and reliability. Following this general evaluation, review individual key competitors qualitatively, covering strengths and weaknesses, share of the market, levels of aggressiveness, and the like. This may take real soul searching, but no one is better qualified to make these evaluations than the division manager responsible for these products or industries. Procedures for competitive analysis are treated in Chapter 3. See Figure 7-4 for an example of the layout.

Facilities Inventory

This analysis progresses from the past to the present. Logically, then, a statement covering the adequacy of existing facilities is in order. This statement should consider not only present conditions but also future needs. This facilities inventory would consider land, buildings, and equipment. Growth plans must anticipate their effect on facilities. This portion of the review highlights present facilities limited for expansion by surrounding properties and old equipment, and perhaps even suggests the need for a new facility at a different location.

Situation Analysis

With the past and present in focus, the **situation analysis** by product is now both possible and logical. One of the first questions might be, "What business are we in?" Although this may sound elementary, it is a question that commands attention. Theodore Levitt, in his "Marketing Myopia" in the *Harvard Business Review*, explored this topic fully, concluding that many companies and industries truly have not defined their businesses properly.[1] For example, does a division supply components to many markets, or does it offer a complete line to a special market? Are there gaps in the product sizes or market coverage, and if so, what can be done to redress the problem? At this point in the analysis, perceptual maps would be appropriate. Scrutinizing each product line within a division tends to eliminate the kind of broad-brush approach that results in generalities. Where one product may be enjoying good market share and acceptance, another may be declining to where it should be discontinued. Pinpointing these trends can be most useful (see Figure 7-5).

Figure 7-4

CORPORATE PLAN

Competitive Analysis

Division________________   In $1,000

Product________________

	Compared with Competition		
Evaluation	Above	Equal	Below
Performance			
Design			
Price			
Distribution			
Completeness			
Delivery			
Other (Describe)			

<u>Competition</u> (Briefly describe each major competitor's importance, detailing their strengths, weaknesses, share of market, aggressiveness, other.)

Competitor A:

Competitor B:

Competitor C:

Competitor D:

Figure 7-5

CORPORATE PLAN

Situation Analysis

Division_________________   In $1,000

Product_______________

<u>Evaluation:</u>

    1. What business are we in?

        a. A component or parts supplier to several markets?

        b. A complete line supplier to limited markets?

    2. Are product lines and/or market coverage complete?

        a. If product lines are incomplete, what should be added?

        b. If market coverage is incomplete, what is the solution?

THE FORECASTS

Following situation analysis, it is time to define and forecast goals for the next several years. In order to do so, consider each product line, with forecasts of orders, shipments, profits, capital expenditures, operating expenses, research and development expenses, and an estimate of the percent of the market sought. Logically, the number of employees should be included, divided into direct and indirect labor. See Figure 7-6 as a format example.

Order Forecasts

Order forecasts are covered in Chapter 5. There are several approaches, and more than one should be used. The field sales organization plays an essential role in this activity. This step must precede any other forecasts. Because the plan is comprehensive, an order forecast by division or business unit, product, and industry is desirable. The responsible manager must review these results carefully. By default, the easy way to forecast is to add a factor for each year, thus projecting continual growth. One must take care that forecasts three or four years out are not just wild guesses. Since all other forecasts (shipments, profits, etc.), depend on the order forecast, it must be as objective as possible. Most business cycles last only four years, a factor worth considering when compiling a five-year forecast.

Besides order level numbers, it is essential to develop qualitative background material, such as reasons for projections of new or improved product, lower costs, and larger available market. Comments on the erosion of present markets, the slippage of products in present markets, and new opportunities should be discussed. The risks involved must be stated along with contingencies to overcome them. The initiatives required to achieve these projections become a significant part of the plan. Acquisitions, price increases, new designs, new customers, or new products may be required to achieve the objectives of top management. It is this part of the plan that must undergo frequent review. The results will translate into the quantitative portions of the plan. In earlier days, these elements were not adequately defined. Since changes in the numbers were not always identifiable by cause, a weak plan resulted.

Figure 7-6

CORPORATE PLAN

Projections

Division________________   In $1,000

Product______________

PRODUCT	1991	1992	1993	1994	1995
New Orders					
Shipments					
Pretax Profits					
Capital Expend.					
R&D					
% of Market					
Employees					
Direct					
Indirect					

Research and Development

Research and development (R&D) expenses can be a major factor in many companies. Sometimes there are communication problems between R&D and marketing, resulting in divergent directions. R&D programs should be detailed, listing their present and projected budgets. As this information integrates with the sales and facilities plans, inequities will surface.

Shipment Forecasts

The shipment forecast emanates from the order forecast. Once inventory levels and production lead times are known, projection of shipments is a direct conversion. This conversion may disclose overly heavy loading of certain plants or departments. Here, too, disparities may emerge. Someone with experience in the manufacturing processes should review the converted data to ensure that it makes sense when compared with historical patterns.

Up to this point, all the activity has been marketing centered. The respective marketing operations even handle the conversion to shipment forecasts, in consultation with manufacturing. Now it is time to turn over these data to the financial people for conversion to profit plans.

Financial Forecasts

Financial projections are necessary at the division or business unit level. Many companies may not attempt profitability estimates for each product. The data consists of many long-range estimates, and forecast errors may be compounded at the product level. Where division or business unit managers have full control from order to billing, they should submit their plans including profit forecasts to the treasurer, through the coordinator. Other groups, responsible only for sales, engineering, and service, should submit their data to the coordinator. After review, the coordinator submits to the financial group for its profit calculations. Final results will include an estimated income statement, source and application of funds statement, and balance sheet.

GROWTH PLANS

With new order, shipment, and profit forecasts available, it is time to use this information to fulfill the company objectives set forth earlier. Forecast results may show that even with optimistic projections, growth is not sufficient for company goals. This may dictate the need for growth through acquisition of other companies or products. If so, the responsible managers should specifically identify the target companies and how they will fit into the objectives.

If growth is from other sources, they should be detailed. The managers should set measurable time schedules. Plans may require organizational changes. They should include consideration of product, industry, facilities, order, and shipment levels. Analyses of forecasted business may verify that company objectives are too optimistic. They also may attest that there is much greater opportunity than ever expected. The possible interpretations and decisions of the input data are legion. Each company must decide for itself the pace and direction from this point forward (see Figure 7-7).

Capital and Facilities Plans

Compiling the **facilities plan** is necessary at this time. The projection of the land, buildings, and equipment needs has progressed with the order forecasts. Marketing gathers this information from the appropriate sources, sharing with manufacturing and other functions the results of the order estimates. Here a reconciliation may be required. If order forecasts were too high for planned facilities, the latter needs adjustment. Conversely, if the order forecast is low, present facilities may be underutilized. Figure 7-8 illustrates a suggested format for recording these plans.

Prepare for Contingencies

So many imponderables and influences impact on the economy and on the individual company that it is impractical to assume that a strategic plan will not change. With this in mind, it is necessary to establish contingencies for unforeseen or unattainable conditions. Some companies prepare more than one plan so that they can retrench to a lower level if necessary. This type of tactic is a time saver, since it anticipates in its preparation the possibility of change. It provides a type of speculative scenario that recognizes that all plans are not achievable in a rapidly changing world.

Figure 7-7

CORPORATE PLAN

Action Plan

Division________________   In $1,000

Product______________

<u>Specific Action:</u>

Based on the assumptions used in the forecast, report in detail.

(e.g., acquisitions, new products, new markets, expanded line, etc.)

Figure 7-8

CORPORATE PLAN

Facilities

Division_________________   In $1,000

Product_______________

Facilities	1991	1992	1993	1994	1995
Property					
Buildings					
Equipment					
Furniture					
Vehicles					
Other					

Identify major items in the above values.
All items in excess of $5,000 are to be capitalized.
Identify whether major items are additions, replacements, or for maintenance.

Follow Up

One reason for detailing the plan by product or industry is to provide enough information for review and measurement. It is possible for the company to meet its plan in total sales and profits, even though some products or divisions perform so poorly that they impede growth. The ability to identify such conditions allows the company to make adjustments throughout the year, fine tuning the plan to get the most out of it. Two of the most important factors in preparing a plan are timeliness and speed. The ability to recognize conditions that provoke change, coupled with the ability to handle corrective action quickly, may mean the difference between profit and loss—or even survival.

In the earlier days of planning, the availability of computerized preparation and modification was limited to the larger companies. Today, personal computers greatly facilitate both preparation and modification. Large spread sheets can be modified quickly, with new results readily available for review and approval. Various scenarios can be posed in a fraction of the time previously required for such exercises. Available software enables planners to use many new techniques. With the amount of number crunching taking place, one of the chief caveats will warn against considering only quantitative data and ignoring qualitative information.

Some consider self-examination and goal-setting as prime benefits of planning. Obviously, not all plans are successful. William Kelly, writing for *Sales & Marketing Management*, listed eight of the most common failings in planning:[2]

1. No coordination—need catalyst for whole endeavor;
2. No valid data—begin plans with reliable guestimates;
3. Historical bias—too much emphasis on history;
4. Inadequate budgets—failure to support with budgets;
5. No field involvement—lack of interchange with field;
6. Rigidity—plans are not straitjackets;
7. Lack of communication—up, down, and laterally; and
8. Poor structure—need well-conceived, relevant format.

Coordination Required

Every planning process needs an individual or committee to oversee the procedure and make certain that the involved people finish their assignments on schedule. Without this coordination, the process drifts and drags interminably. This coordinator is not the chief planner; that is the job of the chief executive. The coordinator is a catalyst.

Valid Data Required

The final plan will only be as good as the data used in developing the history and forecast of the future. If the present situation cannot be determined accurately, the company will be starting from the wrong position and therefore will be saddled with a faulty plan. If the estimate of the future is but a wild guess, the plan has little chance of being more than that.

Historical Bias

Certainly history has a bearing on the company's direction. However, merely to extrapolate historical trends is fraught with danger. If there is one thing that is risky, it is the assumption that the future will replicate the past.

Need Sufficient Budgets

Marketing planning takes the time and effort of high-priced talent, since the real planners are the leaders of the various divisions. Further, to complete most plans there are expenses or capital charges that must not be underestimated. A sound plan presupposes adequate staff and funding.

Involve Field Sales

The field sales organization is an integral part of a realistic forecast. If a company develops all its plans at the home office without any input from the field, it is missing an important element in the process. It is not a question of the field putting its final stamp of approval on a corporate plan, but rather that the plan recognizes and uses its important input.

Allow Flexibility

A rigid plan probably will fail. Changes in the economy, the climate, the organization, the world political situation, and the competition certainly will influence the success of the plan. Any of these factors may cause a change in the direction or timing of the original plan, and thus dictate the need for flexibility.

Proper Communications

Effective communication among the participants is mandatory. This does not mean that lengthy memos should be dispatched in every situation, requiring long meetings and approvals. It does mean that the participants must be active and informed. Members should have access to one another and must be able to settle most questions face-to-face or on the telephone. Clearly, at certain points in the process, all members should know the status and what items still require their action.

Proper Structure

As stated earlier, many viable formats exist, although only one was presented here as an illustration. The format must be achievable and must make sense to the participants. The format must not be so theoretical that it ignores essential qualitative factors. Recent moves in the planning field have placed more emphasis on the manager's planning, rather than on the efforts of staff mathematicians.

SUMMARY

Marketing planning is a critical part of the total corporate plan. Besides beginning the planning cycle, it identifies and generates new product ideas, identifies market opportunities, develops plans on how to penetrate the market, and evaluates the results. Even so, since it is but one part of the corporate plan, it must interface with all the other corporate functions.

Before any planning takes place, the company must clearly identify its mission and objectives. This may require several iterations, since a simple desire for growth is not sufficient. A mission statement can clarify objectives that are not understood consistently by all functions of the business. This in itself is an important benefit.

Planning may take many paths, depending on the present organization of the firm. The basic groupings of product, industry, and geography require slightly different approaches. However, applying the basic steps modified by organizational constraints leads to effective planning.

Every planning activity needs a coordinator, whether it be a department or, in a smaller firm, an individual who has other responsibilities as well. Information must flow in both directions. Further, many questions must be answered concerning technique, intent, timing, delays, and other variables. This coordinating function should report to the chief executive officer of the company.

To establish the proper focus, it is necessary to look at the past and present for a true situation analysis. The tables illustrate the types of useful data. Individual situations will dictate changes to the formats to meet specific problems.

Forecasts of orders, shipments, expenses, development costs, facilities, and the like must precede financial projections. Each functional forecast has its own approaches and problems. The chapter on forecasting addresses many of these. Qualitative comments must be part of the quantitative estimates as substantiation of expectations.

The action plans result from the forecasts. To do otherwise would be planning in a vacuum. The external climate of the marketplace, factored by marketing's plans, must be known prior to any commitment to acquisitions, or major capital expenditures. The financial forecasts, which may well have to be adjusted later, will follow.

An essential component of any plan is follow-up. Reporting on the status of the plan as the year progresses is basic. Adjustments in individual components may be necessary, but the firm should never lose sight of the final objectives. Allowing for contingencies will assist in handling revisions and still permit the ultimate goals.

REFERENCES

1. Levitt, Theodore, "Marketing Myopia," the *Harvard Business Review*, July-August 1960, pp. 45-66.
2. Kelly, William R., "Planning Problems and Pitfalls," *Sales & Marketing Management*, Feb. 6, 1978, p. 31. Reprinted by permission.

8

Sales Compensation

Sales compensation plans require continual review. To make such reviews, the reader should consider the various alternatives. An existing compensation plan may have outlived its effectiveness and may not be achieving today's sales and marketing goals. The following items are significant:

♦ Usual types of compensation plans: straight salary, commission, and combination;

♦ Incentives as components of compensation plans; and

♦ Suggested provisions in establishing pay plans.

Sales compensation plans take many forms, and companies continually seek to improve their programs by trying different approaches. It is common for firms to revise pay plans as circumstances such as the economy, the company structure, or its management undergo change. Although many other benefits accrue, pay plans should be designed to fulfill the company's basic business objectives.

There are three basic types of sales compensation:

1. Straight salary;
2. Straight commission; and
3. Combination plans.

In some respects, compensation is an anomaly. Straight salary values are usually confidential, a status preferred by both the company and the individual. This can be a sensitive subject. On the other hand, incentive income often receives much fanfare, with the recipients honored as winners in a competitive contest. Part of the value of incentives has to do with these visible rewards. The ability to show the prize or discuss the award trip adds value to the program.

STRAIGHT SALARY

This form, as the name implies, consists of a regular wage paid whether sales are high or low and regardless of whether quotas have been met. A chief benefit of this method is easy administration. Since each person's salary is unvarying (except for planned increases), there is no need to monitor individual performances for incentive purposes.

Most salespeople consider themselves professionals, and a regular salary tends to support this perception. Moreover, some like the idea of a predictable income. Many families prefer this to the uncertainty of not knowing what will be in the next paycheck. The company also benefits from the knowledge that it can calculate the chief component of its selling expense. This method also reduces the salesperson's resistance to performing non-selling activities, such as market research or missionary selling.

STRAIGHT COMMISSION

This method provides a variable income for the employee—the antithesis of straight salary. Some employees prefer straight commission because it provides the opportunity to make more money. Salespeople also like the relationship between increased performance and reward. Companies that prefer this method can pay on the basis of sales, lending stability to the expense-to-sales ratio.

Designing a straight commission program requires care. While a company may want to reward good performance, it also should consider the unusual conditions that can skew a commission system. Should there be, for example, a cap on commissions? With some plans, it is possible for the salesperson to make more than the branch manager or regional manager. Unforeseen "windfall" jobs occur sometimes within territories that have made little or no contributions to the projects. Unless rules govern these conditions, an individual could receive a large unearned commission. Some companies exclude U.S. government projects from their commission calculations, since these orders can be substantial and are likely to be managed by home office personnel.

COMBINATION PLANS

The design of these plans unites the best features of straight salary and straight commission plans. This category also includes salary-plus-bonus plans.

Everyone Gains

In the combination plan, the salesperson receives a base salary, with an added incentive for performance. Some companies endeavor to pay salary levels of 80 percent to 90 percent of total estimated income, since even the individual who fails to reach the incentive level accrues a base income. In bad times, when orders are scarce, companies may reduce the risk to the salesperson by raising the base. This type of plan is not easy to administer, but if the result approaches goal, both the company and salesperson benefit.

Meeting Quotas

The commission content of mixed plans usually depends on meeting individual performance goals, or quotas. These may be based on the total of dollars booked or on meeting a predetermined product quota. Bonus content may be tied to a group incentive, where a certain total quota must be met and individuals share in a "bonus pool" based on an announced calculation. Participation in either type is not automatic; it usually requires an agreement from the company that the individual is eligible.

Does the Company Benefit?

Examples of combination plans will be reported later to illustrate their positive and negative features. If the variable component is based on achieving certain levels of individual quotas, a strange condition can occur. Large commissions may be paid to certain salespeople for superior performance, but the company may fall well below its total order plan because the remaining salespeople operated well below target. This is an incentive for some in the sales force, but a misfortune for the company that incurs added costs and does not make the forecast.

Sales Quotas

If used, quotas (sometimes called plans or targets) must be established with great care. When salespeople can influence quota setting and know that their income will be influenced, there is a natural tendency to suppress the quota. Conversely, if management sets goals that are unrealistically high, they serve as a demotivator rather than an incentive. History sometimes acts as a guide in setting quotas, but the assumption that the future replicates the past is usually faulty. Wherever possible, a quota should include both the type of regular business that remains fairly consistent and the project business, identifiable by customer account.

For a quota system to function, salespeople may be assigned specific accounts. When personnel changes occur, the accounts must be transferred to other salespeople to maintain the original total. This is a bit more complex than it sounds. For example, if salesman A left the company, his remaining quota must be transferred to salesman B. Then steps must be taken to see that the actual credit for B includes the new accounts for the remainder of the year.

Another quirk occurs where a branch manager shares in the same program as subordinates. Does the manager's quota represent the sum of the salespeople in that branch office? If the branch in total makes quota, the manager also makes quota, even if some individuals fall below their goals. However, if the branch manager functions only as a senior salesperson, he or she could take the lowest individual quota, assigning higher ones to subordinates. Then, even if the branch did not make its total quota, the manager would participate in the artificially low target.

Incentives

Sales incentive plans are common in the industrial field. In this chapter, the term "incentive" is used to define the added compensation above base salary earned by a salesperson. It can be in cash, merchandise, or in travel. Usually the intent of an incentive is to increase sales and produce more than the incentive program costs. In other words, there should be an incremental gain. But not all companies embrace this philosophy. Some create incentive programs because competition uses them, while others endorse such programs as a reward for high producers. If the incentive's purpose is to increase sales, and sales increases don't match rising expenses, it is time to examine the program. Concern for sales force morale may prolong an incentive program beyond its original intent and usefulness. Programs should be reviewed regularly and not be cast in concrete.

Sales incentives also are used to launch new products or breathe new life into lackluster products, to increase sales per salesperson, to gain new customers, and to penetrate new markets. Company objectives must be clearly defined in these areas. If not, the concentration in the field may be on the wrong objective. For maximum effectiveness programs should be time-specific. A continuing program loses its appeal over many months. Some argue that programs should not coincide with the usual quarterly or annual commission schedules, and should last no longer than four to six months.

Cash Not Always Favored

Although cash is a major and popular incentive, premiums and trips are popular and effective as well. Some believe that the reward should be something that can be displayed (a prize) or discussed (a trip). Since cash can be equated to regular income, a lower performance resulting in less incentive has the effect of a salary cut. Cash awards tend to be put into family funds and spent as household income. A physical prize or trip is obviously outside the usual compensation and thus functions as an added reward. Another benefit of the prize or trip is spousal participation. Prizes are often household items like VCRs or TV sets, selected with and shared with a spouse. Trips typically include the spouse.

Some believe that personal drive to increase commissions serves as the principal driving force and that other incentives are only added inducements. In other words, incentives are only for extraordinary performance. Still, the incentive and compensation specialists who run programs for companies are significant. Some provide complete programs, including catalogs and sets of rules, and supply the prizes to the winners.

Alternative Approaches to Incentives

1. The interested sales manager can design his own program, supply catalogs, and arrange for prizes. This is not an easy task, since it involves writing the rules, arranging for prizes, keeping score, and ensuring prompt delivery of awards to the winners.

2. The next alternative is to turn over the handling of awards to a limited incentive supply house. This type of organization arranges for catalogs and sees that winners receive their prizes. They often share their experience on the do's and don'ts of prize incentives.

3. The most expensive and least taxing to the sales manager involves turning over the entire program to a specialized organization. Since there are many problems associated with coordinating the details and even more difficulties created by poor travel arrangements, turning over at least part of the program likely will result in a more effective plan. The effect of achieving incentive can be nullified by poor service in awarding prizes (and making adjustments when the prizes are defective or damaged). An award of a trip can be a disaster if airline tickets or hotel arrangements are less than promised.

INCENTIVE PLAN EXAMPLES

There appear to be as many types of payment plans as there are companies who sponsor them. The following types are very popular:

Shipment-Based

Some companies tie incentives to shipments rather than orders. The philosophy is that incentives will be paid when the company receives payment from the customer. On short lead time products, this procedure makes little difference since order and shipment occur almost simultaneously. Some firms limit all credit specifically to the product, deducting amounts for freight, returned goods, sales policy adjustments, and traded-in products. These points must be made clear in the incentive agreement.

Expenses-Based

Incentive payments may be tied to expense control. In addition to a base salary, the bonus is an incentive for keeping costs in check. For example, assume branch office operating costs amount to 15 percent of sales. (This is near the commission rate a rep earns.) Multiplying total orders by 15 percent creates a theoretical commission for the branch office. At year end, if those commissions exceed the total expenses of the office, the excess is considered a pool of bonus money for that office. Distribution of this pool may be handled in different ways: in proportion to each person's orders; evenly among all; at the discretion of the sales manager; or some combination. This plan could be based on orders or shipments.

Product-Mix-Based

Another method assigns a different multiplier to each product line. If the product's factor is 2.0, the salesperson receives credit for twice the value of the order. Some firms use this method to push certain lines. On the other hand, some products may have factors in the range of 0.5, meaning the credit is for half the value of the order. With this approach, the company attempts to control the product mix by rewarding salespeople accordingly. Outside purchases (products purchased from others and combined with the base product) normally have lower factors than company manufactured products. Orders or shipments could form the basis for credit. The company pays a base salary and provides incentive in cash for reaching a minimum quota. Any discounts offered by the home office must be shared by the salesperson.

Customer-Based

The plan may be tied to type of customer. Instead of different factors for each product, the factors depend on whether the orders are from users, house accounts, OEM (original equipment manufacturers), new accounts, or special target accounts. In each case, order values multiplied by a predetermined, published factor set the total credit level for the year. The accumulated credits determine the bonus payment. Orders or shipments may be used as the basis of record. This is similar in its execution to applying factors to products as described on the previous page.

Dollar-Value-Based

Another type of plan assigns credit to each salesperson based on the value of orders booked and compares the credits to quotas established at the beginning of the year. Each major account has a targeted order level based on history and factored with judgment. The quotas, therefore, have substance. Each salesperson receives a salary of 90 percent of an agreed total. Salespeople who do not meet quota receive the 90 percent level as straight salary. However, for exceeding quota, the percentage over quota applies to the salary level as a cash payment. This plan normally operates on a new order basis and provides for monthly payments. It is purely an individual incentive. Since the salesperson is involved in quota setting, there is a sense of participation in the process.

Bonus-Pool-Based

Another bonus plan (in addition to salary) accumulates a regional pool, combining branches into regions. Bonus factors apply to different products based on the company's desire to weight them. There is no specific quota to achieve. For example, small products may have a multiplier of 0.6 percent and larger products a multiplier of 0.3 percent. This is a group incentive, in that the orders accumulate by branch into a regional total. The payments reflect the judgment of the regional managers, subject to the approval of the field sales manager.

SUGGESTED PLAN PROVISIONS

In order to forestall later problems, it is mandatory to provide all participants with the plan rules and ensure that they understand them. The following points are significant:

Timing of Payments Must Be Clear

With a commission plan or a combination plan that includes commissions, monthly payments are the norm. Payments may lag bookings by one month, depending on the time required to close the books and make the necessary calculations. Quarterly payments are not uncommon and tend to negate the impact of short-term aberrations in booking values. The quarterly system also reduces the number of cycles requiring calculations.

Annual payments are more appropriate to a salary-plus-bonus program, where the salary sustains the individual throughout the year, and the bonus represents a performance incentive. Annual payments typically are delayed until the company books are closed and final payments have been declared by the company and verified by the recipients. The recipients generally seem to keep personal sets of books and know exactly how much they have earned. It often requires verification of every order of a particular salesperson to resolve differences.

Plans Must Be Defined in Writing

Defining compensation plans in writing will eliminate confusion over qualifying criteria, method of payment, and limitations. These issues should be settled in advance, especially when they involve non-selling assignments. For example, the firm may need market research on a new product, new market, or new application. Salespeople paid on commission may be reluctant to accept assignments that reduce selling time and therefore their ability to earn income. Under a straight salary plan this is not a problem and in fact is part of the "professionalism" required to handle varied assignments.

Identify the Arbiter

The rules covering compensation procedures also should identify the final arbiter in the event of disagreement between company and employee. This referee is usually the highest ranking manager of the sales division. It is surprising how often this option must be invoked.

Credit Allocation

Credit allocation procedures also must be included in the incentive document. In the business marketplace, it is common to involve several offices in securing an order. These may include those responsible for the customer placing the order (origin), the customer of final installation (user), and a third or fourth party who may influence the purchase. Defining this credit allocation is a necessary function. There are many combinations of credit, and each company must define its own formula. Some companies do not split credit within offices, while some assign credit for all orders, and others split credit only above certain dollar limits. Table 8-1 lists a suggested combination. There are many others.

Table 8-1   Typical Credit Splits

Pre-order sales effort		50%
Receipt of formal order		25%
Prepare & submit quotation	5%	
Receipt of formal order	10%	
Post-order handling	5%	
Territory of installation		25%
Location of installation	10%	
Service responsibility	15%	

These credits may all accrue to one salesperson or may be split among several. Credit allocation disputes are not uncommon. Regional managers usually resolve them, but sometimes they must be settled at the home office level. Salespeople should not try to persuade customers to divert orders in an attempt to acquire undeserved credit. This ploy represents a serious breach of ethics, subject to disciplinary action.

Duration of the Plan

Another statement should address the duration of the plan. Specify the termination date, if one exists. In any case, include a statement indicating that the plan may be revised or terminated at the convenience of the company.

Employee Terminations

A related condition may occur if a salesperson leaves the company. Some plans include clauses that salespersons forfeit incentives if they voluntarily terminate before receiving payment. Further, if a salesperson leaves the company before all accounts are settled, that person may owe money to the company for prior overpayments. This could occur if an incentive was paid on an order that later was declared invalid or was cancelled before the salesperson had earned enough additional credits to offset it. Other companies agree to pay all salaries and incentives earned up to the point of termination.

Order Cancellations

Another consideration involves order cancellations. A cancelled order should be deleted from the credit already assigned to a salesperson. However, an order entered in December 1990 and cancelled in February 1991 raises the question of whether the deduction should be applied to 1990 or 1991. For incentives already paid for December, it would be necessary to deduct the credit in February, perhaps resulting in negative bookings for that month. Moreover, if that individual left the company, he or she would owe the company the value of incentive paid but not earned. This can create a sticky situation. Such conditions actually do occur, and the procedure should be documented clearly in the incentive agreement. Lack of a clear understanding by both parties could encourage unethical behavior.

Each company must decide whether it will have an incentive ceiling or cap. Some impose limits on this amount, while others allow for no limits at all.

Multiple Plans

A company may maintain concurrently more than one incentive plan. This may occur if large products or projects are better covered by a different plan than the smaller, more standard products or projects. In fact, some companies have more than one sales force and thus maintain different incentive plans for each. The company must decide on its own objectives for the sales organization, both to maximize orders and to reward salespeople fairly. A company that sells some products through its own sales force and some indirectly through distributors or reps is likely to maintain more than one compensation plan.

Contests

Contests for the sales organization are a form of short-term compensation. They may be as short as a month to stimulate sales in a low period. A key rule involves the closing date of the contest. A specific cut-off time must be established. For example, the cut-off should be linked to an order's arrival in the home office—not when mailed, not when the customer promises it, and not when it is received in the branch office.

SUMMARY

Sales compensation interests more than sales account representatives. It affects a major marketing expense, influences the drive and morale of the sales force, and may be a factor in attracting applicants to the company. There is no single, best program that applies to all firms and for all products. Companies must pick and choose, using plans that meet specific needs of the day. It is common to turn to new plans as times change. Adjust the plan to the circumstances—not the circumstances to the plan.

The preponderance of industrial companies use salary or salary plus commission or bonus. This confirms the notion that regular salaries are important to professional salespeople in this field. While added incentive for higher performance encourages the salesperson, it allows the company to handle the costs on an incremental basis. Straight salary is a fixed cost, while the expense of incentives varies with the sales level.

Salary levels usually are competitive within an industry and often are targeted at 80 percent to 90 percent of total income for a salesperson. This provides a subsistence wage while challenging the individual to perform at more than an average level. The remainder of compensation is incentive, which may take the form of cash, merchandise prizes, or vacation trips. There is an entire industry devoted to providing incentive services to companies. Those who develop or revise incentive plans should be aware of and familiar with the services available.

As a performance incentive, **cash still appears to be the favored reward.** Some say it does not provide the drive but becomes an expected part of income, while others prefer it to catalog prizes. The latter sometimes lose their appeal when the same prizes are offered every year for the same level of performance. Trips to exotic vacation spots have obvious appeal. However, since the number of expensive trips awarded by any company may be limited, they often go to the same superior people. This lowers the expectations of the less effective individuals, and the incentive value drive may be lost.

Incentives may be based on orders or shipments. They may be individual or group-based, and may be paid monthly, quarterly, or annually. It is essential for the company to keep accurate records of sales. (The salespeople will.) To pay promptly and accurately is the sign of a well-run plan.

Designing a plan requires consideration of many factors. Eligibility, duration of plan, credit splits, products included (or excluded), government orders, ceilings, price levels, and discounts, are examples of items that must be spelled out in the issuance of the plan document. These topics will be raised at some point; it is better to address them at inception. When further questions arise, it shows all is not clear, and these questions should be covered as well. The plan document should be distributed to all eligible participants.

Often, what appears a workable and equitable plan turns out to be a morale shaker, leading to grumbling and less than optimum sales effort. Any change in a compensation plan may meet with resistance because it hits where it hurts—in the pocketbook. If a plan is not working, the company should modify its inequities before they trigger wholesale resignations.

9

Marketing Cost

Careful management continually monitors marketing costs. The pressure to expand "order getting" capacity is pervasive. To some, reducing marketing spending is tantamount to downsizing the organization. The goal must be to get effective results from the amount spent. This chapter covers:

- The components of marketing costs;

- The need for marketing cost information and how to use it;

- Analysis of the major functional departments in marketing; and

- Some suggested methods for controlling marketing costs.

Wat is this mysterious and elusive but significant expense called "marketing cost"? Is it the cost of the field sales force? Is it advertising expense? **It is both and more.** Because marketing elements are so diverse, a useful analysis of their costs and their control can be difficult.

DEFINITION

Marketing cost is the sum of several major marketing categories. Since different functions are represented, measurements and controls must also differ. The following groups, typically headed by a vice president of marketing, make up this expense:

1. Field sales;
2. Advertising and public relations;
3. Headquarters marketing; and
4. Distribution.

Although each has its own identifiable expense, there is another major cost, namely **allocated expense.** Marketing cost is the sum of these five expense categories. Each will be discussed in turn.

1. **Field sales** staffing consists of non-headquarters personnel, including managers, salespeople, and branch office support people. A branch office is defined as any field office, despite its size or composition. This group includes not only the company's direct sales force but also manufacturers' representatives, distributors, and manufacturers' agents who receive commissions for their services. These indirect channels may accumulate costs differently, as will be described later.

2. **Advertising and public relations** constitute a major expense. Sometimes called "corporate communications," this group may include advertising, exhibits, public relations, art department, media buying, audiovisual, and other analogous functions. A major differentiation among companies is whether inside people or outside agencies provide these services.

3. **Headquarters marketing** consists of the following departments: product planning, market research, marketing administration, and industry and product support. This group may be more difficult to

define because company organizations differ. Some companies may combine all non-field activities into one group and call it "home office marketing."

4. **Distribution** is growing in stature and cost today. It often includes order entry, order service, traffic, warehousing, inventory control, and company fleet trucks. The question becomes whether some of these are marketing or manufacturing categories. Because they represent such a large segment of total cost, they must be defined and grouped properly.

Allocated expense is not a direct expense and thus may appear unplanned. For example, how much of the company president's time and expense should be considered marketing expense? In some companies, a president and his staff may devote considerable time to marketing issues. Because of this effort, the company may prosper to a greater degree than one whose chief executive is not as dedicated to marketing. Allocations may come from the executive group, data processing, or engineering, to name a few.

COST MEASUREMENT

Obviously, the delineation of marketing expenses into consistent categories is difficult. It is not that individual expenses cannot be determined; it is a question of how they should be distributed among the various groups. There are many ways to accumulate and report these expenses. It is also easy to compare quickly one's own marketing expenses with published ratios. However, with different definitions, these comparisons require care, or they will be far off the mark.

To control marketing cost, we must measure it. There are many different types of cost. Marketing theory, when defining costs, nearly always contains a discussion of **natural accounts,** such as rent, salaries, travel, supplies, etc. Some companies use the **functional account** approach, namely grouping expenses into transportation, selling, advertising, market research, and other activities. A combination of the two is desirable.

Also, the theory discusses:

(a) **direct costs,** which are obvious;

(b) **traceable common costs,** which can be determined but not easily grouped properly; and

(c) **non-traceable common costs,** or hidden costs, which are difficult to identify. An example of the latter would be the cost of losing a good customer because of late delivery. How can you measure this loss? The theory is necessary and the terminology extremely valuable, but in themselves do not define par or how to achieve it.

The analyst should compile budgets containing the natural accounts **within functions.** This provides a chart of accounts, including salaries, travel, fringe benefits, supplies, and the like. Each department (function), if recorded this way, has a history and a base for planning. Allocations can be added to these expenses. A later chapter will deal with budgetary analysis and control.

NEED AND USE

Sometimes marketing cost analysis gets lost in a company's downsizing efforts. In such instances, the importance of regular analysis becomes secondary to overall cost reduction. Yes, marketing cost analysis should be a continuing operation, not abandoned as a panic solution to a transitory problem.

Field Sales

Consider the following analyses of the **field sales** group:

- Relative growth of expense;
- Customer call patterns;
- Size and location of field sales force;
- Sales per salesperson;
- Incentive programs;
- Field sales budgets; and
- Control.

Relative Growth

While accelerating expenses should be evident, they often are neglected. The question is: How fast is selling expense growing relative to company orders? In some cases, profit volume as well as order volume should be used for comparison. Selling expense may be growing rapidly due to a resurgence in business or because of a new product introduction. These conditions may dictate a continued high level of expense for the immediate future. However, in a mature company with established products and markets, if selling cost is rising faster than company sales or profit, it suggests something is amiss and needs correction. For adequate comparisons, information should be collected not only on the company but on total industry expenses and orders.

Customer Call Patterns

The field sales group needs expense information to plan call patterns and frequency. This subject is treated in greater detail in another chapter. It is extremely costly for salespeople to call haphazardly on customers or try to cover every customer, large or small. With the cost of an industrial sales call exceeding $250, it is too expensive to operate without proper controls. At $250 per call, you cannot call on all customers. There will be customers whose potential is too low for regular calls. These must be handled by telephone, direct mail, or some other effective approach.

Size and Location of Field Sales Force

Good marketing cost data helps determine sales force size and location. The expense budget limits sales force size. Location of salespeople raises another question: Should they be dispersed evenly throughout the country, centered in major cities, or assigned on another basis? Major customer locations set the geographic concentration of potential. These statistics are available from government publications, industry reports, and trade associations.

Sales Per Salesperson

How much should the average salesperson book in orders? Some companies expect salespeople to sell more than $1 million per year, while others expect much lower values. This depends on the company, product, territory, experience, and other variables. Determining par for comparison by industry is difficult yet necessary if the expense analysis is for control of selling expense.

Incentive Programs

Incentive payments for salespeople are part of selling expense. Incentives are designed to stimulate orders. Yet it is possible for a company to pay individual incentives, and not meet total order plans. Also, since these payments may be made on an annual basis, they may be difficult to estimate. Conversely, incentives may be too low to retain good people. The influence on expense and morale can't be underestimated.

Field Sales Budgets

Selling cost information helps decide expense budgets. The cost of maintaining a salesperson in the field must be known. Otherwise, budget preparation consists of taking last year's actual expense and adding a factor. This perpetuates inefficiency and inequity. Poor past performance likely will generate poor future performance.

To calculate selling expense for field sales, start from ground zero and build up individual items in the chart of accounts based on knowledge, not guesses. For example, for a branch sales office budget, estimate the amount for salaries, travel expense, supplies, etc. Salaries are for known people. For other expenses, use history factored by good judgment. The values must be based on a realistic assessment of efficient operations.

When these expenses are totaled, convert that value to a **direct cost** per person. See Table 9-1 for a comparison of how this is done for direct and support people. The average cost per person is a valuable tool for estimating increases in budgets when offices need new salespeople or support people. The indirect expense also will rise with an increase in personnel but not in direct proportion.

A review of individual expenses highlights the big spenders within a sales force, as well as those who spend too little. Some companies encourage their salespeople always to take lunch with customers, since 11 a.m. until 1 p.m. is prime selling time. The available time a salesperson can see a customer equals about six hours per day. Thus, these prime two hours in mid-day represent one-third of the available work day. It is good business for a salesperson to spend this concentrated, uninterrupted time with a customer. If one branch office uses this approach and another does not, the former may appear to have higher expenses. However, when comparing the two by order level, the story can be sharply different.

Table 9-1

BRANCH OFFICE EXPENSES
In Dollars

	Total All Office Exp.	Direct Expense			
		Total Office Exp.	Each Acct. Rep.	Each Support	Each Secretary
Compensation	222,000	222,000	55,000	35,000	22,000
Fringes	55,500	55,500	13,750	8,750	5,500
Travel	14,900	14,900	4,800	500	
Entertainment	6,300	6,300	2,000	300	
Auto Lease	12,600	12,600	4,200		
Other Auto Exp.	9,000	9,000	3,000		
Communications	29,300				
Postage	2,100				
Rent	20,000				
All Other Exp.	6,300				
Total Expense	378,000	320,300	82,750	44,550	27,500

This office consists of three salespersons, three support, and one secretary.
There is sufficient office room to add two more people.
Communication expense: telephone, fax, telex, computer linkage to home office.
All other expenses consist of the remainder of small accounts.
Direct expenses equal 85% of total expenses.

Control

Sales managers should review and approve expense reports, call reports, trip reports, customer visits, and other activities of their people. This will ensure compliance with company guidelines and policies. Left to their own devices, branch managers may succumb to the daily time pressures and neglect this assignment.

ADVERTISING AND PUBLIC RELATIONS

Another major expense in marketing is for advertising and public relations, sometimes known as corporate communications or mass selling. This is a dominant expense in many companies, often generating the largest single indirect expense related to selling. As a large account, advertising stands out sharply within the marketing division budget.

There are several ways to calculate advertising budgets. The following discussion covers the more popular.

1. The **percentage of sales** approach sets the budget at some predetermined percentage such as 2 percent or 3 percent of total sales volume. Therefore, as sales rise the advertising budget rises as well. While this is the simplest approach and the most popular, it is not necessarily the best. It fails to address such issues as new product promotion, new catalogs, new identities, etc. It also assumes that advertising should remain a constant percentage, no matter what the level of sales. Also, many advertising managers are reluctant to cut budgets when sales decline, contending that when sales are down, advertising should increase. This method also assumes that sales generate advertising, rather than the reverse.

2. **Matching competition** provides another approach to advertising budgets. Although this may appear to be keeping up with the market, it ignores the marketing need. It assumes that the competition knows the market, and matching its efforts ensures proper coverage. This approach is not recommended.

3. **The arbitrary method** is another imprudent approach. It involves merely guessing at the appropriate budget. This is experience based with no real need determination. Most managements would

question this from the start. The budget is so large that management wants logical justification.

4. A better method is the **task approach,** which estimates expenses for identified requirements, or tasks. When totaled, the company may find such a promotion too costly. Thus, to reduce expenses the least significant projects can be deleted. Conversely, budgets for unusual expenses can be provided for: new product introductions, major trade shows, acquisitions, etc. Making these judgments may be difficult, and thus this approach is sometimes avoided.

No single measure indicates precisely how much advertising a company should plan. It depends on the product, company, image, management, and a combination of these. Where 2 percent of sales may be adequate for one company, 4 percent to 5 percent of sales may be necessary for another. It is essential, therefore, to gather detailed information on expenses for various tasks. This allows building the budget on specific needs.

There is also a question of how to assign advertising expenses by product or department. Many product managers believe that corporate advertising fails to meet their needs. Naturally, all would like considerably more attention, such as more representation in publications and press releases. Good marketing cost control makes it possible to allocate the advertising budget across product lines based upon their usage and need, not their sales volume. A new product introduction may require extensive pioneer advertising, while an established product needs only retentive advertising to remind customers of availability and product excellence.

HEADQUARTERS MARKETING

The home-office marketing group is a staff function for support of line sales operations. As a diverse organization, it is difficult to measure their specific contribution. There is no question of their need. Without planning, research, forecasting, and the like, the sales division would have no direction. But how does one measure the contribution in dollars that can translate to need for numbers of people? Typical organizations would consist of the following:

Marketing Administration

This department often defines overall policy and creates the strategic marketing plan. This department must have a total view of the company mission, beyond marketing objectives. The marketing manager must have close connections with corporate managers, sales managers, and other division chiefs. Strategic planning obviously requires input from many sources. Thus marketing managers must be proven communicators.

Product Planning

Product planning, in the marketing sense, is the second arm of new product development. Research and development, often credited with all new product concepts, constitutes the other arm. Product planners must work close to the market. They must know the competition. They must know customer wants and needs (not always the same). In short, they are marketing technologists.

Industry and Product Support

Personnel in this department provide essential technical support for the field sales force. Complex products require technical people to understand and explain product operation to the field and to customers. Often these company experts visit customer locations to provide enlightenment on product performance. Their work involves recruiting new customers or reinforcing the loyalty of existing customers. Organization builders may question whether these people belong in marketing or in the product and industry divisions. Their trips to the field, often requested by the sales group, pose a budgetary problem of who pays for their travel. If they must respond to the requests of sales, they have no control over their own budgets. Yet the sales group requires them for their performance.

Market Research

Market research is an operation often misunderstood and sometimes considered an "ivory tower" kind of activity, devoid of the practicalities of good business operation. However, market research people must be thoroughly conversant with both the market and the product. They provide the marketing division with marketplace data.

DISTRIBUTION

Companies are organized differently to handle these essential logistical functions. Combining them in one group makes sense when they are considered as in-house, post-order activities. These activities occur after the order is booked and before it is shipped.

Order Entry

Order entry has varied locations. Some companies, believing that sales should control the order, want this function associated with sales. Others perceive it as a manufacturing responsibility. Still others want it divorced from both and thus identified as headquarters marketing.

Manual order entry rapidly is yielding to **electronic entry.** With computers in the field offices, and even in customer offices that have access to the central computer, electronic entry is becoming increasingly popular. Converting to electronic order entry takes great care and attention. Orders entered improperly due to poor programming, careless entry from the field, or inattention at the home office create major customer relations problems. But once installed and running, electronic entry is faster and more accurate than its manual alternative. It should be the goal in every company.

Order Service

Order service exists separately in some companies and may combine with order entry in others. It is mentioned here for those interested in keeping them separate. This group deals with customers and field sales—after order definition but before shipment. Order service provides a central location for post-order information. As with order entry, the product or industry groups sometimes want control of this activity. Some companies leave the order service function in marketing for standard products, but transfer complex products to product or industry divisions.

Traffic

Traffic deals with shipment of the product. Orders may be shipped by land, sea, or air; prepaid or collect; and F.O.B. or F.A.S., to name a few combinations. Traffic works out these details with customers and arranges for the carrier. The value of this service probably is more visible to customers than to suppliers.

Warehousing and Inventory Control

These distribution functions closely relate to manufacturing. Arranging for storage of completed products certainly is within the province of the distribution group. This is a part of their shipment scheduling. Control of inventory of standard products for quick shipment also falls within this department. The need for close cooperation is obvious.

ALLOCATED EXPENSES

Allocated expenses often create contention. Expenses such as utilities are not always identifiable by department. Taxes or rent expense must be allocated. The allocation of common space, such as hallways, may be questioned. However, these costs must be absorbed proportionately by marketing and thus must be recognized. The measure of how they are proportioned is the usual stumbling block.

Sales managers often insist that they need more support from the headquarters sales group or from advertising. When informed of the size of these allocated expenses, they are surprised. In some companies, sales managers must "purchase" these services from the staff departments, and they want the most for their money.

CONTROL OF THE COSTS

The above review of the cost generators provides an understanding of their origin and function. This knowledge permits analysis and suggests areas of better control.

Direct Field Sales Expense

The expense for field sales links itself to many comparisons. History defines actual expense and actual orders. Calculate the expense to orders ratio (E/O) for each year and chart it. Also chart the history of orders. An example is shown in Figure 9-1. This chart tells a story. Any sharp movement should be explainable. In this example, the E/O ratio jumped in 1989

Figure 9-1 Orders and Expense/Order Ratio

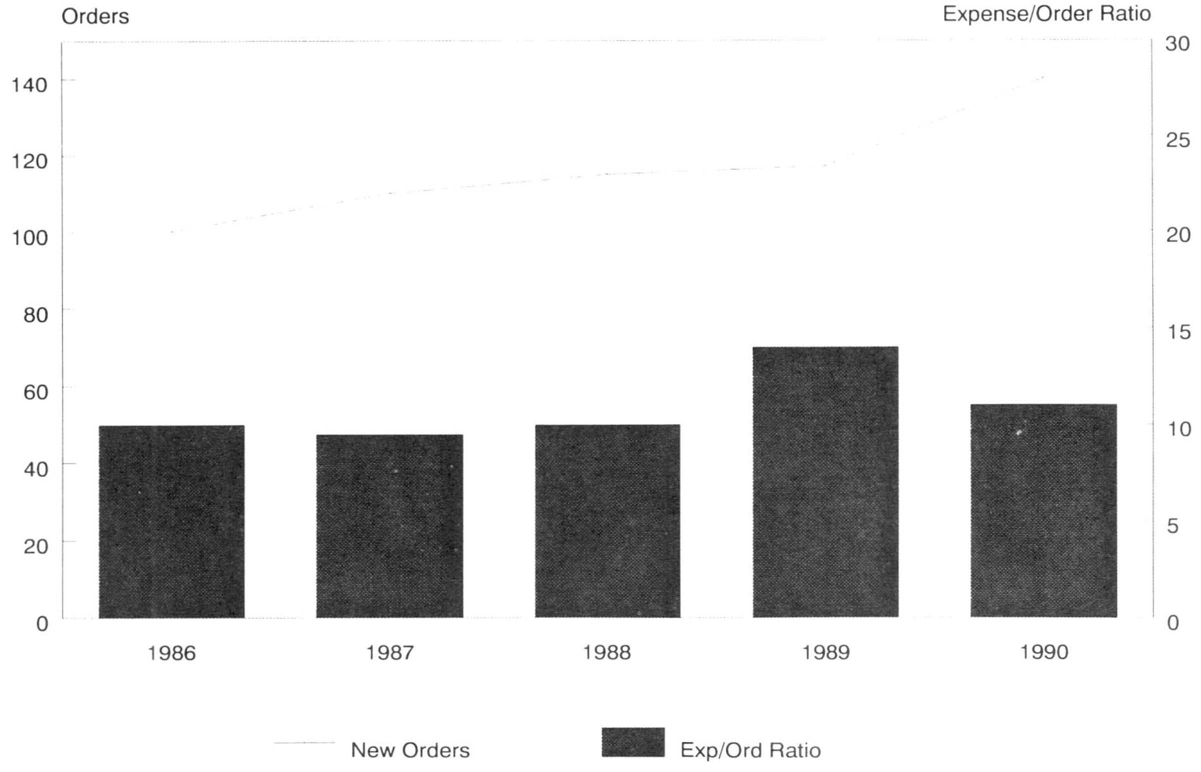

due to an increased sales force to handle a new product. In 1990, the effect of the new product showed in the order volume. Changes in distribution channels (direct versus indirect), new branch offices, and new products all can influence cost, at least temporarily. Changes in expense and order patterns should acknowledge changes in distribution.

Also relevant is the method of record-keeping. Ensure that your data remain consistent over the years. Record-keeping often changes, even with the same terminology. Note the following:

a. Managers may be included in administration in some years and in sales departments in others.
b. Acquisitions may have been folded into order totals, although sales organizations may differ.
c. Accounting may have changed its costing procedures.

The importance of a consistent and well defined E/O ratio is evident when trying to compare with industry totals. *Sales & Marketing Management* publishes data on sales expenses and states clearly they are direct expenses.[2] These include compensation, travel, and entertainment expenses only. If your costs include depreciation and office rent, they will not match. However, if you use the *S&MM* studies, adjust your data properly. **It is extremely important to know your data well.**

Indirect Field Expense

Handling the cost of indirect distribution is another area of potential discrepancy. Many companies use distributors and manufacturers' representatives (reps) for all or part of their selling. This can pose problems when trade or professional associations essay marketing cost studies. Companies may bill their distributors or reps at list price less their commission. This reduces the income to the company. Further, since these intermediaries are not on the payroll, they are not in the field sales expense budgets. Does this distort your E/O figures? In the final income statements, it is common to add these commissions to selling expense and to the sales value. This adjustment may not be done in daily or monthly order statistics for analysis purposes. **Be careful.**

A significant difference in expense may result when using reps versus your own sales force. Reps' commissions may run 15 percent to 20 percent, where your own force may have an E/O of only 10 percent. However, the former may be preferable in a low potential area where it may be unprofitable to maintain a branch office. Channels of distribution are discussed in more detail in another chapter. Here note that the costs between channels may be significant.

Cost Per Sales Call

Another analytical tool is the cost per sales call. The chapter on call reports covers this subject in detail. You may build a history and compare your present performance against the past. Again, it is essential that definitions be consistent. *Sales & Marketing Management* also publishes data on call costs for industrial companies.[3] The same caveats apply as stated earlier on the use of outside data. See Figure 9-2 for a sample format.

Figure 9-3 presents a simple yet effective analytical tool. This chart compares travel and entertainment expense by individual salesperson for each month of the current year. Changes stand out sharply for review. Branch and regional managers find this type of report very valuable in terms of regular expense control. Travel and entertainment expense also lends itself to comparison with outside data, such as that published by *S&MM*.

These tools are fundamental to good marketing cost control. They provide historical comparisons and are amenable to comparisons with published sources. Trade associations may provide similar data. If not, this would be an appropriate suggestion for their statistical group. These results may indicate a need to lower expenses. On the other hand, they may reflect a good, tightly controlled, efficient sales force.

ADVERTISING EXPENSE

Advertising expense is a large, necessary cost that comes under fire from many quarters. No matter what the value, many people believe it is too high. Documentation of the content through the task approach confirms the need for the expense. New product bulletins, trade shows, regular advertising, and public relations all can be documented with specific costs. Any of these can be reduced, but the effect on company image or on sales must be considered. Some measurements of advertising effectiveness may be imprecise, but there is little disagreement that advertising is necessary. Cost documentation is essential, since justification of charges is often necessary.

Advertising managers must know the marketplace. They should reach their target markets with the appropriate media, working closely with sales to identify markets and customers. Knowing what the competition is

Figure 9-2

HISTORY OF SELLING EXPENSE
Jan–Dec

	1985	1986	1987	1988	1989	1990
Number of						
Reg & Br Mgrs						
Account Reps						
Support						
Secretaries						
Total Personnel						
Total Orders						
Total Expenses						
Orders/Acct Rep						
Expense/Acct Rep						
Calls/Acct Rep						
Expense/Call						

Notes: Regional and branch managers are included in total expenses.
Incentive payments are included in total expenses.
Orders, expenses, and calls per account rep exclude managers.

Figure 9-3

TRAVEL AND ENTERTAINMENT
1990 EXPENSES

	Jan	Feb	Mar	Apr	May	Jun	Jul	Aug	Sep	Oct	Nov	Dec	YTD
BOSTON													
Jones													
Smith													
Jackson													
Tot Boston													
CHICAGO													
Kane													
Jarvis													
Webster													
Porter													
Tot Chicago													
NEW YORK													
Thomas													
Nolan													
Lee													
Hoffman													
Palombo													
Watson													
Tot New York													
LOS ANGELES													
Carver													
Chisholm													
Marshall													
Sawyer													
Newman													
Robbins													
Tot Los Angeles													
TOTAL TRAV & ENT													

spending can be helpful. The 10K reports required by the federal government annually are public information and readily available. Request them from your competitors' treasurers. These reports list advertising expense as a separate item in one schedule. Take care when comparing this information to your own values because of definitions. However, these data do provide some guidance.

Create Services or Buy Them?

The use of inside services versus purchased outside services is the subject of continuing controversy. Some companies maintain minimal inside departments that act as coordinators with outside agencies who provide all services. In other companies large inside organizations perform nearly every relevant function. The philosophy of corporate management is usually the determinant in such matters. Having information on the cost of these alternatives provides advertising management a ready tool for documenting costs and recommendations.

HEADQUARTERS MARKETING

This third major group in the marketing organization generally functions in a staff capacity.

Marketing Administration

As a staff group, they must possess exemplary communication skills. Depth is required for product knowledge, corporate vision, internal political conditions, and market sensitivity. Communication skills are essential in dealings with all levels of the company hierarchy. Management must be confident of marketing's ability to generate and help execute the strategic plans. These skills should be reviewed and bolstered where necessary. Marketing director is a key position.

Product Planning

Product planning should be reviewed for customer and market knowledge. This group also must relate well with research and development. New product work requires the close coordination of marketing and R&D. This work also entails risk. Fear of failure of new products is common. Some people become so hesitant that they only want to work on extensions of **present** products, thus sidestepping the risks inherent in a **new** product. Human problems are often greater than suspected in this activity. The manager must be aware of how timidity may affect cost and performance.

Market Research

Market research people must stay current with the state-of-the-art. Membership in trade groups, trade associations, and marketing councils should be encouraged for the invaluable contacts. Cross-fertilization of ideas and techniques cut costs. Performing studies as they were carried out ten years ago may be easy, but it's an expensive route to follow. New data sources must be explored continually. New software comes on the market regularly. **This group must keep up-to-date.**

Industry/Product Support

Industry/product support requires promptness and good customer relations. Questions from customers need quick response. Good customers can be lost to poor attitudes. While it is necessary to have good application knowledge, it's also necessary to translate that knowledge into effective customer service. Some companies assign people to telephones or computer stations. Customer support rewards companies who handle the function well.

DISTRIBUTION

The responsibility for distribution moves between other functions depending on the present company organization. No matter where it reports, its duties are essentially the same.

Order Entry

Most companies are trying to reduce order cycle time, which starts with order entry. Electronic order entry systems are replacing manual systems, even in smaller companies. Investigate to see if these are performing as promised. Down time, programming errors, or complicated procedures increase cycle time and errors. Be sure the operators are computer literate.

Order Service

Order service personnel are the first line of post-order customer contact. Companies must not tolerate cavalier attitudes toward customers. Customers call or write because they have questions or problems. Admittedly these questions interrupt other duties, but in its service function, this group must be responsive. Hidden costs of doing business originate here.

Traffic, Warehousing, and Inventory

These, like most of the distribution group, must respond quickly to post-order problems. While some company personnel identify only the sales force as customer contact points, the people staffing headquarters marketing make an equal contribution to the efficacy of customer relations.

SUMMARY

Consistency of data has been mentioned several times. Whether compiling data for internal comparisons or gathering it from outside, **know your data.** Proper definitions prevent comparisons between unlike quantities.

Make internal comparisons first. Be careful of comparing selling expense and orders of direct sales offices with expenses and orders of reps. You can make analyses, but make sure you know the content of the direct versus the indirect.

In comparisons between branch offices, don't limit your study to orders booked. Your salespeople may have been heavily involved in writing specifications or favorably influencing the customer in one location. However, the customer may have placed the order from a different location. Make sure that user or influence credit are counted.

Continual review of marketing cost is necessary. History may show sharp changes in orders or expenses. These changes usually can be identified. They may include new product introductions, recession, restructuring, or other changes. Look for patterns.

Reorganizations play havoc with statistical data. Extrapolating from a territorial organization to an industry focus changes many of the ground rules. People may be transferred between the field and home office. Others may find themselves reporting to a manager halfway across the country. Don't try to evaluate both organizations with the same yardstick.

Marketing cost analysis is an essential function. Understand each of the functions in the marketing department and how their expenses vary.

You may need to record these expenses down to the individual level. Analysis must be qualitative as well as quantitative. There is much behind the raw numbers. People problems are significant. There is no question of the importance of marketing expense—but only a question of how to best measure it and implement the results.

REFERENCES

1. "1991 Sales Manager's Budget Planner," *Sales & Marketing Management*, June 17, 1991, p. 72.
2. Ibid. p. 5.
3. Ibid. p. 72.

10

Expense Budgets

Marketing expense budgets must reflect the impact of qualitative factors in their preparation, review, and control. The economy, competition, and new products, to name a few, are all variables that influence the marketing focus. A standard addition over last year's budget does not satisfy these needs. This chapter covers the following:

- Significant marketing expenses;
- Need for defining the budget cycles;
- Steps in preparing a marketing budget;
- The importance of regular budget review; and
- The need for confidentiality and consistency.

Where forecasts estimate the order flow coming into the company, the expense budget controls the money spent to obtain those orders. An expense budget is as vital as a forecast. Plans, call reports, and other types of control devices depend on expense control. Without a formal budgeting process, expenses just happen, and their correction and control depend on chance. Conversely, if budgets are so rigid that they preclude adjustments and corrections, sales and marketing may be limited in their ability to take advantage of changing conditions.

This discussion focuses on the expense budgets of the sales and marketing operations, although the comments may apply equally well to other divisions. This qualification reflects the interrelationships among accounts and the importance that must be assigned to certain expenses.

The significance of salaries, travel and entertainment, and communication expenses will be highlighted in this chapter. The discussion will concentrate on direct expenses. Allocated expense to sales and marketing from other operations such as engineering, data processing, etc., are less controllable and must be negotiated with those organizations. The costs of salaries, travel, and communications can easily amount to more than 90 percent of total direct marketing expense.

It is necessary to know and control the natural accounts of salaries, travel, supplies, communications, etc. However, for better control it is necessary to assign these expenses to functions such as branch office, industry, or product so that each can be isolated and examined in terms of performance against budget.

Salaries

In a sales and marketing organization, the largest single recurring direct expense is salaries, including fringe benefits. This account may represent 70 percent of a department's direct expenses. Therefore, the number of people is significant. This is often the first consideration in reducing costs during a restructuring.

Travel and Related Expense

The next largest expense is usually for travel, including customer entertainment, personal meals, leased automobiles, and other auto expenses. Each of these categories may be handled as a separate account. These accounts require continued scrutiny. There are internal solutions, such as having one's own travel department, that minimize these costs.

Communications

Another significant expense is for communications, including telephone, Telex, mail, and any other communication expense charged to the department. In these days of electronic order entry and electronic mail, such costs tend to rise sharply, and there is little history available for guidance.

Charts of Accounts

Accounting departments define the various accounts used in collecting and reporting expenses in a "chart of accounts." This provides documentation and definition of how expenses should be categorized. However, due to changes in organizations and methods of doing business, the precise definitions of the categories do not always filter through to the marketing people. Further, the chart of accounts may be couched in accounting language not necessarily understood by marketing people. Therefore, the marketing organization should compile a set of approved definitions in marketing language. This list, which should be sent to those who receive budget reports, need only cover the accounts normally charged to sales and marketing. This glossary saves much time and effort with consistent definitions.

BUDGET SCHEDULES

Before compiling an expense budget, the timing cycle of the budget periods must be set. If the company uses a calendar month basis, there will be different numbers of weeks in the months and quarters, sometimes making comparisons with prior periods difficult. Also, working days per month may vary from nineteen to twenty-three. This 21 percent differential may reflect in reports of actual expenses per month. Holidays and vacation shutdowns also will influence this figure. Some companies shut down for maintenance either during the summer or at year end. This practice may reduce the number of working days in those months to fourteen. Cost saving measures also may prompt companies to work with reduced staffs during certain periods.

One way to resolve these variables is to work on a four- four-five week calendar. In this method, each quarter contains thirteen weeks, the first two months each having four weeks, and the last month of the quarter having five weeks. Although company personnel recognize that the months may not end on the last day of the calendar month, the gain in consistency offsets this problem. A special calendar should be prepared with this information. Still another approach allows for a thirteenth month to capture those late December expenses not received into the accounting department until early January.

Budget Revisions

It really is not enough to establish a budget at the start of the year and consider the job finished. There should be reviews at least quarterly to compare actual expenses against budget. This is also a time to factor in any changes that may have occurred in the business environment since the preparation of the original budget. It is possible that the total economy, industry, and company business have improved over earlier expectations. Here the forecasts and budgets should be adjusted to compensate for these changes.

If business suddenly declines, downward corrections must be made to expense budgets. With a quarterly review, such corrections can be made quickly. When making a review, it is customary in many companies to review not only the remaining quarters in the year but to add quarters of the following year so that they are always looking four quarters ahead. Quarterly results do not come as surprises for those companies that issue expense control statements monthly. These statements give even earlier warnings of situational changes.

Somewhat related to the previous discussion on the need for definitions is the establishment of a liaison between the accounting and marketing organizations. It is convenient to assign for this purpose an individual or small group which works closely with the marketing staff, but understands the accounting parlance required to handle this function. Since marketing and accounting tend to think differently due to their specific duties and training, this interface can gain the confidence of both. It is not really an additional layer of organization but an opportunity for one person to be part of two organizations concurrently—like an interpreter.

Baseline Expenses

In budget development, bases must be assigned for the amounts projected for each account and each department. Department managers tend to ask for high budgets for fear of falling short and receiving unfavorable judgments by their superiors. It is usually better to fall below a budget than to exceed one.

With established departments, it is relatively easy to estimate a total for the following year. History is a good guide here. However, certain guidelines are necessary, such as the personnel level, average proposed salary increases, and expected changes in other large accounts. Senior management customarily issues these guidelines.

New or reorganized departments with no history present a different problem. General guidelines may be useful, such as average travel costs (salaries being a known factor), rental costs, communications, and the like. Some of these may come from analyses of other departments in the sales operation. (Also see "1991 Sales Manager's Budget Planner," published by *Sales and Marketing Management*.)

PREPARING A BUDGET

The following is an illustration of budget preparation for the coming year, where calculations are made in October:

1. Compile the history of the department through September of the current year.
2. Assume no change in the personnel level.
3. Target average salary increases at 6 percent. (An annual salary increase of 6 percent per person translates to a total salary increase of 3 percent, since increases occur throughout the year.)
4. Estimate fringe benefits at 25 percent of salaries. (These include vacation pay, insurance, etc., and will rise with salaries.)
5. Expect communication-related expenses to increase 5 percent (due to increased computer transmission between the field and home office, telephone expenses, and postage).
6. Allocate data processing to increase by 6 percent (due to new programming for automated quotation and order entry systems).
7. Estimate travel-related expense to increase 10 percent.
8. Assume all other expenses will remain the same.

Figure 10-1 portrays the process. Note that an account "all other" covers the other expenses, many of which are individually small. This calculation simply develops a reasonable department total for approval purposes.

Following approval of totals, all finite accounts can be developed to fit within the department total. The accounts listed in Figure 10-1 amount to 98 perent of the current year's expenses and thus are adequate for estimat-

Figure 10-1

BUDGET CALCULATIONS
SALES DIVISION

ACCOUNT	9 MONTH ACTUAL	3 MONTH ESTIMATE	TOTAL YEAR	FACTOR	NEXT YEAR
Salaries	$200,000	$66,667	$266,667	1.03	$274,700
Fringes	50,000	16,667	66,667	1.03	68,700
Travel	6,700	2,300	9,000	1.10	9,900
Entertainment	3,400	1,100	4,500	1.10	5,000
Personal Meals	1,200	400	1,600	1.10	1,800
Auto Lease	9,000	3,000	12,000	1.10	13,200
Other Auto Expense	6,700	2,300	9,000	1.10	9,900
Telephone	20,300	6,700	27,000	1.05	28,400
Postage	2,100	700	2,800	1.05	2,900
Communication	9,000	3,000	12,000	1.05	12,600
Data Processing	1,800	600	2,400	1.06	2,500
All Other	6,350	2,100	8,450		8,500
TOTAL EXPENSE	316,550	105,534	422,084		438,100

Note: Values for next year are rounded.

ing totals. Also note that in the next year, the estimates are rounded off. Later it will be easier to work in thousands when analyzing and correcting the results. It is unlikely that the preliminary estimate for any one account will be within $100 over an entire year. Any large increases should be documented and justified to help the management in its approval review.

Review Salaries and Fringes Monthly

A refinement can be added to this type of estimate. Accounts such as salaries and fringes should be reviewed for the latest month. That month may be higher than the nine-month average, since salary increases may have occurred in August and September. Since these are fixed expenses, the last three months should be calculated as three times the latest month. One must be careful not to do this with all accounts, because monthly aberrations are common in travel, entertainment, and other large accounts.

When all departments have been estimated and the totals approved, final budgets can be prepared using all the accounts. This means breaking out the detail in the "all other" category. Preliminary department totals must be maintained. Department managers must be a part of this final reconciliation, since they are responsible for meeting budgets in total and by account.

Divide Total Budget into Quarters

The final budget should be divided into quarters. Some companies do this merely by dividing the totals by four. Other companies try to recognize the differences in quarters by factoring in their quarterly planned salary increases and identifying quarters where other unusual expenses will occur. Heavy expenses can be targeted, e.g., sales meetings, added personnel, office relocation, and employee moving expense. Recognizing these expected outlays in the quarterly budgets allows for better comparisons with actual numbers when these larger-than-usual expenses do occur.

Use Personal Computers

This division budget, which may include many departments, can be prepared on a personal computer. Individual departments may be combined into a field total or other grouping, and again subdivided as necessary. Any last-minute revisions (and there are usually many), may be calculated conveniently. If the final consolidation does not agree with the preliminary, a comparison by account will usually bring the discrepancy to light.

Use Staff Department

Marketing budgets typically include a staff department that covers top sales and marketing managers. This department includes their salaries and expenses along with other major costs not controlled by any other department. These can be significant expenses, not normally approved at the branch or department level. Examples would include reserve for the incentive plan, employee moving expenses, and major allocations not applicable to individual operating departments. Therefore, it is simpler to provide that budget in the staff department and accumulate actual expenses there as well. The top sales and marketing manager usually controls the staff department budget personally.

Confidentiality

This is an important consideration in preparing budgets. Salaries are strictly confidential, and few people in the company have access to them. Obviously this material requires discreet handling. Because of this, small departments may be combined to eliminate the possibility of someone "backing into" salary figures where they should not have access. If a department has only two or three people, it is relatively simple to estimate each person's salary. Thus the need for combining departments for budget purposes.

Need for Flexibility

It may sound contradictory, but budget procedures should be flexible. For example, transfers are common within a division, or even between divisions, and procedures should allow revisions to budgets and actuals to accommodate these transfers. Such changes do not affect the total expenses of the company but only the division charged. Also, with today's computerized processes, expenses are sometimes coded incorrectly, thus charging the wrong account or department. Computer programs should allow adjustments for such corrections. Sometimes these programs are so rigid that simple adjustments become major problems.

BUDGET REVIEWS

With a properly prepared budget tested under actual operating conditions, it is time to look beyond procedures. The information is more important than the process.

Monthly Reviews

Actual expense versus budget should be reviewed each month. This should begin at the consolidated level to determine whether the entire organization is operating within budget for the month and year-to-date. If not, the consolidated review gives a quick picture of the trouble spots. Accounts that are decidedly above or below budget point to a review of the individual departments for problem areas. It may be a "one shot" charge in a single department, which is explicable and proper, or it may be a continuous overrun. The latter may be due to additional personnel or just lack of control. In any case, it highlights an area needing correction.

Review Individual Departments

All departments need individual review since these are the responsibility of managers whose performances may be judged by their ability to control expenses. Here again, it requires care to analyze and correct improper charges if they exist. It is much simpler to observe and correct these charges as they occur than to recreate the situation many months later.

Track Major Costs Regularly

Other useful analyses involve monthly tracking of major costs such as personnel levels and travel expenses. Chapter 9 on marketing costs provides illustrative charts showing how these may be tracked. The chart on travel expense (Figure 10-2), is repeated in this chapter for confirmation on how to control expense budgets. Besides being a chief reason for overruns, this expense often provides insight to other expenses that are running out of control.

Figure 10-2

TRAVEL AND ENTERTAINMENT
1990 EXPENSES

	Jan	Feb	Mar	Apr	May	Jun	Jul	Aug	Sep	Oct	Nov	Dec	YTD
BOSTON													
Jones													
Smith													
Jackson													
Tot Boston													
CHICAGO													
Kane													
Jarvis													
Webster													
Porter													
Tot Chicago													
NEW YORK													
Thomas													
Nolan													
Lee													
Hoffman													
Palombo													
Watson													
Tot New York													
LOS ANGELES													
Carver													
Chisholm													
Marshall													
Sawyer													
Newman													
Robbins													
Tot Los Angeles													
TOTAL TRAV & ENT													

SUMMARY

Budgetary control often reverts to accounting departments, with marketing departments merely accepting the results without question. In truth, marketing should be involved actively in preparation, analysis, review and control. To abdicate this responsibility is to settle for a quantitative process that may not recognize the many qualitative factors involved.

Marketing organizations must understand their spending. Unbridled expenses mean lower profits for the company. On the other hand, enough must be spent to get the job done. It takes spending to get orders—the question revolves around how much to spend. The ratio of expense to orders described in Chapter 9 is a good measure here. It is a measure of efficiency. If that ratio compares favorably with industry norms, there is a sense of operating in the right range. If the ratio is too high, it signals the need for study and corrective action.

It is important for marketing personnel to recognize the importance of certain accounts in the overall scheme of cost control. Otherwise, inordinate emphasis may be placed on controlling the cost of minor items such as paper clips. Salaries, fringes, travel-related costs, and communication expenses are large contributors to the total expense. Review and control them as a first step.

Comparisons with prior years or prior months require a consistent reporting calendar. Whether a company operates on a true calendar month and year, or whether it operates on four thirteen-week quarters is important in reviewing costs. Quarterly budget preparation must be done carefully, to prevent disproportionate values from occurring.

Preparing a budget requires history, or at least a knowledge of important accounts and their relationships. The chart in Figure 10-1 provides a simple yet workable method of preparation. This can be done easily on a personal computer and modified as conditions change.

Confidentiality is important to marketing personnel and to the company. The number of people with access to the budgets—and particularly the salary figures—must be limited. Where necessary, it may require combining smaller departments to maintain this confidentiality.

Some computerized budget programs do not provide for easy adjustments for improper charges made to accounts or departments. Also, the many changes that occur in sales and marketing departments require the ability to handle revisions promptly. If department managers believe they are losing control of their budgets because of stringent computer programs, their attention to detail will wane.

Finally, actual expenses must be compared to budgets monthly. Corrections can be made promptly and cognizant managers made to feel like participants if these comparisons are continual. Do not let comparisons slide for several months; adjustments may never rectify the original problems correctly.

11

Marketing Audit

To audit is to examine. Such examination may point to corrective action or may confirm good marketing health. In either case, the audit is a necessary review. The chief factors are contained in this chapter:

- The importance of marketing self-examination;
- The usual audit approaches, external and internal;
- The organizational position of the auditor; and
- The need to report the results.

The term "marketing audit" does not imply impropriety. It does denote investigation, an internal review of the status quo, similar to an accounting audit. It should be a regular review to ensure that procedures are proper and consistent, and that data is handled correctly. Like a regular physical examination, it often can head off trouble before it occurs.

A marketing audit may concentrate on one area, such as marketing cost, or it may involve a complete review of all marketing activities. Different companies handle their audits according to their needs. Ideally an audit will be a regular review, with the expressed intent to adapt marketing activities to changing conditions. An audit may be conducted by an outside organization or internally by someone who enjoys the confidence of both management and the marketing people. If conducted by an insider, that individual should be someone outside the marketing division who can bring objectivity to the study.

Normally marketing audits consist of two elements: external and internal reviews. The external section studies the environment, or the climate surrounding the company, while the internal audit analyzes the operations within the company. Both are necessary, a fact not always recognized.

EXTERNAL FACTORS

A review of the business environment will put the results in focus. This becomes an analysis of what might be called the "uncontrollables," or fields not under the direct control of the marketing manager. These can be classified as follows:

- Economic–demographic;

- Technological;

- Political–legal; and

- Social–cultural.

1. **Economic** forces play a major role in the business of any company. Tight money and a lagging economy create a much different climate than booming business conditions at the peak of the business cycle. This must be recognized in forecasting and planning. Looking only at the near-term history may result in rash decisions.

Recent economic slides have been blamed on beliefs that major downturns are things of the past. This is not true. Qualitative factors have a major influence on business.

Demographic shifts also have a profound effect. Corporate expansions and diversifications cause shifts in industrial concentration, causing entirely new commercial and business centers to emerge. These dynamic changes affect the location and staffing of industrial sales branch offices that serve those businesses.

2. **Technology** changes daily. The development and growth of new products has created entire new markets. Some of these new products have not only created new customers but have changed the way business is done internally. The personal computer is a classic example. Computerized quotations and order entry, almost unheard of ten years ago, are now commonplace. New processes continually are being developed to take advantage of new equipment, and the market for new products grows accordingly. Since the demand for new products also may obsolete existing products, it is a cycle that demands constant attention.

3. **Political and legal** changes depend on the incumbent government, either local or national. Strictly enforced laws affect the company and the economy. Increases in taxes or in reporting requirements normally affect the business community adversely. Some presidential policies have been more strict than others in enforcing the national statutes. Some states have the reputation of being more favorable for business investment.

Sometimes the emphasis on certain factors may be a burden on one company but represent a boon to others. For example, heavy emphasis on pollution control will cost some companies additional facilities and money while simultaneously increasing the market for companies selling that type of equipment.

4. **Social** changes in the consumer market can create demands for changed products in the industrial field. As the introduction pointed out, industrial markets are derived from consumer demand. Also, there are times when there is an unfavorable sentiment in society about certain businesses, e.g., chemical plants. It may take major public relations and advertising efforts to reverse this feeling.

5. **Competition** is a further external consideration that merits review. This has been covered in some detail in Chapter 3. Let it be acknowledged that competitive analysis is a consideration in the marketing audit.

INTERNAL FACTORS

The internal portion of the audit should cover the activities discussed in earlier chapters, namely:

- Information systems;

- Product analysis;

- Competition;

- Distribution channels;

- Forecasting;

- Call reporting;

- Planning;

- Sales compensation;

- Marketing cost; and

- Expense budgets.

Another important area in the marketing audit is the study of **customers.** This continuing analysis is part of the overall corporate picture. Mergers and acquisitions have created new companies with new names, and have caused some company names to disappear. It is essential that major customers be tracked and their dossiers kept current. Today it is not unusual for a company to be acquired, almost lose its identity, then be cut loose again as an independent with new or perhaps the same original owners. Changes in customer organizations may lead to new decision makers, new preferences for suppliers, or even worse, ownership by competitors. This may change the entire complexion of plans for the future and may dictate a whole new approach to the market if some of these customers are unusually significant.

Situation Analysis

Following the examination of internal and external factors, it is possible to analyze the situation as to:

1. What has happened;
2. Why did it happen; and
3. What to do about it.

1. The external world may be in deep recession or in a state of war. These conditions may dry up the market for some products and might stimulate the market for others. Or, it may be a time of business growth calling for expansion. Internally the company may have grown in good times and now be oversize for the business at hand. Combinations of these conditions call for different solutions.

2. Orders for industrial products often experience large swings as the economy moves through its cycles. It is not always easy to determine if the reasons are due to strong competition, the health of the economy, poor product, or delivery performance. Sometimes the economy alone appears to be the culprit, but companies more frequently are looking inward for the solutions. (See *The Wall Street Journal* article, May 29, 1991, pp. B1-2, entitled "Akers to IBM Employees: Wake Up!")[1]

3. Internal and external problems must be identified. There may be no control over the external, but recognition allows adjustments for the conditions. Whether internal or external, create a plan for action. Hoping and doing nothing probably will exacerbate the problems. Even a healthy company requires frequent internal and external reviews.

While the answers may differ with the company and the conditions, they can at least provide direction. No two companies will conduct their audits in the same way, nor will their conclusions likely be comparable. Some examples of conditions that are not always evident but are likely to emerge from an audit include:

♦ The development of a new product that replaces an earlier one, where the price of the new product is lower. This would result in fewer dollars for the same or better product performance. Although the sales dollars may be lower, the profits should be higher.

♦ A change in the company's policies that would create a new shut-down period, for example, the first two weeks in July. This may be mandatory, thus reducing the number of working days in that month and year. Although the situation may be recognized, the audit should highlight and quantify the change.

- ◆ A realignment of territories, due either to a reorganization or a shift in customer locations. This can distort historical patterns and therefore distort expectations.

- ◆ The defections of salespeople may be a sign of trouble. If the company appears listless and does not provide opportunities for salespeople to sell and make money, they will leave.

SUMMARY

The importance of a marketing audit now should be evident. It should be conducted regularly, not just to cure a panic situation. Internal studies should be covered as well as external. Unfortunately, many companies continue to look outside the organization for their solutions, when an internal review may provide the real answers. The auditor may be from outside the company or from within. If the latter, take care that the individual or group is truly neutral without allegiance to any department. If an outside company does the audit, careful supervision is necessary to prevent a standardized answer to your specific problems. The auditors must understand your company and people, and not merely feed back to you what you already know.

Interviews must be conducted with the departments involved to get an impression of the actual conditions. These interviews should begin at the top corporate level and progress downward. Respondents should not feel threatened, but should believe that their input is important to the company direction and operation. A complete report should result from the audit. It should identify the situation as it exists, highlight any problems that surface, and suggest solutions. Some solutions will be obvious, but others will emerge from a study of the whole picture. The marketing audit might trigger major decisions for the direction of the company. It is well worth the effort.

REFERENCES

1.   Carroll, Paul B., "Akers to IBM Employees: Wake Up!", *The Wall Street Journal*, 29 May 1991, pp. B1-2.

12

Report Presentation

Marketing reports should be designed for the reader. The most expansive report is worthless if it is unclear. Certain readers prefer particular formats for tables and graphs. The reader is your customer and deserves to be served. Consider the following factors:

- Readers need consistency of presentation;
- Tables and charts should be clear and simple;
- Output must be accurate to earn management confidence; and
- Report value is often measured by timeliness.

The preceding chapters dealt with the analysis and management of the marketing organization. What do you do with this information? Corporate and sales managements are often skeptical of revolutionary approaches that promise to reinvent the wheel. Sometimes it is frustrating to develop an approach that would "obviously" benefit the company. Where management lacks enthusiasm, younger practitioners might become discouraged.

Presentation, then, becomes the key. Warmed-over solutions are unwelcome. Similarly, a sophisticated mathematical approach can meet with a lukewarm reception because it does not fit the present chemistry or philosophy of the company. This was evident in the early days of personal computers when some managers avoided computers because of a sense of personal inadequacy or the mistaken idea that these were tools for secretaries and accountants.

Courses in verbal presentations are extremely popular, and properly so. Presentation skills are essential for anyone aspiring to achieve management status.

Presentations to departmental peers or higher levels of management are routine and require careful preparation. However, some individuals consistently present ideas to management literally on the backs of envelopes, with little thought given to appearance or appeal. There are, of course, emergency situations where this might be necessary. This author once presented a longhand forecast summary to senior management in a crisis situation where the single page was thereafter referenced as "that yellow sheet forecast summary."

Be Consistent

As creatures of habit, we tend to make verbal presentations in the same manner. However, charts and reports too often are assembled haphazardly. Give your reports a family resemblance. In time, your recipients will recognize your reports by their form and content, even without your identification. On historical tables, do you put the earliest data on the left and progress to the right, as on a graph? Or, for emphasis, do you put the latest information first on the left and work backward to the right? When you do both, you create confusion.

What Does Your Management Want?

Marketing and general management require certain information to run their operations. Since time is precious, it's not a matter of what you *want* to show but of what they *need* to know. These are not mutually exclusive. First and foremost, find out what management needs to know:

♦ Are new orders up or down by month and year-to-date?

♦ Why are they up or down?

♦ Are you comparing to last month, last year, or the trend?

♦ What extenuating circumstances caused the present situation?

It is always important in presenting recommendations to answer the question, "Compared to what?" Orders may be up in the month for many reasons: it might be the last month of the quarter, a large contract may have been entered, a price increase may be pending, or a new product may have been introduced. These factors are not always obvious to all readers. Although these conditions may compare unfavorably to last year, this does not suggest one should hedge the facts; present them as they are, answering why.

Historical order tables by month and quarter answer many questions. If your reader wants to review the same month's performance over several years or compare quarters or look at the progression over the current year, that information is all available. Refer to Table 12-1 for a suggested format. You are not forcing a format but presenting enough information to answer questions. Without a proper format, you may be asked how certain figures compare with last year. You may be asked, "Was it really a good month?" or "How do we look year-to-date?" A single page of total company orders answers all of these questions.

Extenuating Circumstances

Large orders are common in the industrial equipment business. Unfortunately, memories are short with reference to when they occurred. List the major orders that unduly influence order totals. Long lists explain why certain months are large, just as short lists show why orders were low. It is difficult for any management to recall whether a particular order's entry date was March or April when reviewing data in the third quarter. Such lists also should include major cancellations, if any, because of their influence.

Table 12-1

ORDERS BY MONTH
HISTORICAL REVIEW
In Million $

	1985	1986	1987	1988	1989	1990	1991
Jan.	80	82	72	74	90	80	75
Feb.	76	78	72	84	84	78	80
Mar.	84	86	90	84	100	78	84
Apr.	74	80	84	80	96	74	
May	80	84	86	82	90	84	
Jun.	90	92	102	100	96	102	
Jul.	70	70	74	80	70	64	
Aug.	78	76	78	84	74	66	
Sep.	96	100	102	100	98	100	
Oct.	80	82	94	96	90	88	
Nov.	80	80	90	88	86	84	
Dec.	94	90	92	120	110	116	
YTD	982	1,000	1,036	1,072	1,084	1,014	239
1st Q	240	246	234	242	274	236	239
2nd Q	244	256	272	262	282	260	
3rd Q	244	246	254	264	242	230	
4th Q	254	252	276	304	286	288	

Note: Values are fictitious—for illustration only.

Year-to-Date versus Monthly Data

Any single month may be distorted by the occurrences mentioned above. Such analysis has been likened to reading the newspaper for only one day and trying to understand the world situation. Year-to-date information tends to be smoothed by the peaks and valleys of order entry. If the forecast reflects seasonality, this is even more important. Table 12-2 provides your readers with the best of both worlds. The monthly orders are

Table 12-2

ORDERS BY INDUSTRY
CURRENT MONTH
In Million $

INDUSTRY	Sept. Actual	YTD Actual	YTD Forecast	YTD $ Var	YTD % Var
Mining	2.8	20.0	18	(2)	(11)
Food & Kindred	12.4	90.0	90	0	0
Textile	4.1	30.0	32	2	6
Paper & Allied	12.4	90.0	89	(1)	(1)
Chemical	8.3	60.0	55	(5)	(9)
Petroleum	8.3	60.0	62	2	3
Rubber	2.8	20.0	20	0	0
Stone, Clay & Glass	5.5	40.0	37	(3)	(8)
Primary Metals	5.5	40.0	35	(5)	(14)
Fab Metal Products	4.1	30.0	25	(5)	(20)
Machinery ex. Elec.	6.3	46.0	43	(3)	(7)
Electrical Machinery	5.5	40.0	39	(1)	(3)
Transport Equipment	4.1	30.0	35	5	14
Utilities	11.0	80.0	85	5	6
Government	6.9	50.0	53	3	6
TOTAL	100.0	726.0	718.0	(8)	(1)

Notes: Values are fictitious—for illustration only.
      ( ) indicates negative value.

reported as information, but the comparisons with forecast are on a year-to-date basis. Here again, many questions have been anticipated.

Matrix Tables

Often, two groups need to be compared. The need to know how each product is penetrating geographical markets begins to get into the detail of what is truly happening. Table 12-3 presents a matrix of product orders versus regional office on a year-to-date basis, both compared with forecast. The responsible marketing groups have their information, and general management sees the influence on total company operations. Such tables can be prepared to compare any of the principal groups.

Table 12-3

ORDERS—REGION & PRODUCT
January–September
In Million $

	North-east	South-east	Central	South-west	Pacific	Total Product	Product Forecast
Motors	10	6	10	8	6	40	38
Pumps	4	4	7	7	5	27	25
Pulleys	9	10	8	6	7	40	37
Controls	15	15	20	30	20	100	95
Boilers	8	7	8	10	7	40	43
Ovens	17	14	13	11	10	65	67
Region Total	63	56	66	72	55	312	305
Region Fcst	60	50	65	70	60	305	

Note: Values are fictitious—for illustration only.

Trust in the Data

Management's belief and trust in the reporting is essential. Sometimes rapid and important decisions depend on monthly information. The old saying of carpenters, "measure twice and cut once," may be paraphrased as "investigate twice and report once." This trust needs to be built on proven output. Marketing reports and recommendations must engender the same trust that management has in the accounting operations.

Report Format

Prepare reports that are consistent in appearance. They may have special facings or covers that immediately identify your operation. Eventually they may be known by the cover color, e.g., "Green Book" or "Blue Book."

The first page should be a one-page summary, preferably with a chart, stating the results of the month and year-to-date. A glance at this page tells the big story, while the supporting details follow on subsequent pages. Do not discourage your readers with bulky reports. Your aim should be to create a document that will stay on their desks as a ready reference.

Establish a consistent distribution list. If the material is sensitive and should be limited, ask the chief user to establish the list. Often certain employees want to receive information they do not require. That decision should be left to the principal user.

Timeliness is essential. The data processing schedule may not release composite reports for several days after month end. The advent of personal computers makes it simple for marketing departments to issue "Flash Reports" almost immediately on order totals. This may be all that is required for an early analysis. If business is bad or declining, management will want returns, even if preliminary, as soon as possible.

SUMMARY

Make your reports consistent, clear, and accurate. Poor photocopies, varied formats, and questionable data make them worthless. Let the managers decide what they need, then create reports or recommendations that will make it easy for them to use. It is very gratifying to hear, "This is not what I asked for, but it is exactly what I need."

Bibliography

Andrews, Kenneth R., "Strategic Planning of Mice and Men," *Across the Board*, Nov. 1983, pp. 6-9.

Bailey, Earl, *Getting Closer to the Customer* (Research Bulletin No. 229), New York, NY: The Conference Board, 1989.

Bailey, Earl, *Competitive Leverage* (Report No. 876), New York, NY: The Conference Board, 1985.

Bailey, Earl, *Marketing-Cost Ratios of U.S. Manufacturers* (Report No. 662), New York, NY: The Conference Board, 1975.

Battaglia, Greg, "Strategic Information Planning," *Information Executive*, Winter 1991, pp. 54-56.

Bertrand, Kate, "The 12 Cardinal Sins of Compensation," *Business Marketing*, Sept. 1989, p. 51.

Block, Robert S., "Ten Commandments for New Product Development," *Industrial Research/Development*, Mar. 1979, pp. 97-100.

Buchin, Stanley, and Davidson, Timothy, "Computer-Aided Sales Forecasting," *Business Marketing*, Aug. 1983, pp. 75-81.

Bylinsky, George, "Turning R&D Into Real Products," *Fortune*, July 2, 1990, pp. 72-77.

Cardinale, Richard, "User Involvement—An Assessment of the Need for the Vital Link in the Systems Development Process," *Information Executive*, Fall 1990, pp. 37-39.

Cespedes, Frank, and Corey, E. Raymond, "Managing Multiple Channels," *Business Horizons*, Jul.-Aug. 1990, pp. 67-76.

Choffroy, Jean Marie, and Lilien, Gary L., "Strategies Behind the Successful Industrial Product Launch," *Business Marketing*, Nov. 1984, pp. 82-94.

"Corporate Planning: Piercing Future Fog," *Business Week* (Special Report), Apr. 25, 1975, pp. 46-54.

"Correlation Between United States and International Standard Industrial Classifications," Technical Paper 20, U.S. Department of Commerce.

Couretas, John, "Most Plans to Boost Spending; Cash Tops the List," *Business Marketing*, Apr. 1985, pp. 40-46.

Crawford, C. Merle, *New Products Management*, 3rd ed., Homewood, IL: Richard D. Irwin, Inc., 1991.

Cymbala, Robert J., "How Good Information Can Feed the Strategic Planning Process," *International Management*, Apr. 1984, pp. 62-64.

DeWolf, John W., "A Simple Do-It-Yourself Approach to Forecasting Your Business Cycles," *Business Marketing*, Oct. 1983, pp. 96-100.

Fahner, Hal, "Call Reports That Tell It All," *Sales & Marketing Management*, Nov. 12, 1984, pp. 50-52.

Falvey, Jack, "There's No Call For Call Reports," *Sales & Marketing Management*, Nov. 1989, pp. 122-123.

Gregory, William E., Jr., "Time to Ask Hard-Nosed Questions," *Sales & Marketing Management*, Oct. 1989, pp. 88-93.

Grupe, Fritz H., "Planning Your Expert System Strategy," *Information Executive*, Winter 1991, pp. 46-49.

Helmeke, Todd M., "Strategic Business Unit Market Planning" *Business Marketing*, Nov. 1984, pp. 43-55.

Hill, Christopher T., and Utterback, James M., "The Dynamics of Product and Process Innovation," *Management Review*, Jan. 1980, pp. 14-20.

Hopkins, David, *New Product Winners and Losers* (Report No. 773), New York, NY: The Conference Board, 1980.

Hutt, Michael D., and Speh, Thomas W., *Business Marketing Management,* New York, NY: The Dryden Press, 3rd ed., 1989.

Jenks, James M., "Executive Consensus: Non-Computer Forecasting Approaches to Use Right Now," *Business Marketing,* Aug. 1983, pp. 82-84.

Kent, Debra, "PCs, TVs or CBs? What's Hot in Sales Incentives," *Business Marketing,* Apr. 1985, pp. 57-64.

Kuczmarski, Thomas D., *Marketing New Products,* Englewood Cliffs, NJ: Prentice-Hall, Inc., 1988.

Lele, Meline, "Matching Your Channels to Your Product Life Cycle," *Business Marketing,* Dec. 1986, pp. 61-69.

Levitt, Theodore, "Marketing Success Through Differentiation—of Anything," *Harvard Business Review,* Jan.-Feb. 1980, pp. 83-91.

Levitt, Theodore, "After the Sale Is Over," *Harvard Business Review,* Sept.-Oct. 1983, pp. 87-91.

Levy, Robert, "Innovate or Replicate," *Dun's Review,* June 1980, pp. 87-91.

Maher, Philip, "Corporate Espionage: When Market Research Goes Too Far," *Business Marketing,* Oct. 1984, pp. 51-66.

Main, Jeremy, "Help and Hype in the New-Product Game," *Fortune,* Feb. 7, 1983, pp. 60-64.

Marken, G.A., "How to Get the Most Exposure for Your Next New Product," *Business Marketing,* Nov. 1983, pp. 104-110.

Mellow, Craig, "The Best Source of Competitive Intelligence," *Sales & Marketing Management,* Dec. 1989, pp. 24-29.

Moriarty, Rowland, and Moran, Ursala, "Managing Hybrid Marketing Systems," *Harvard Business Review,* Nov.-Dec. 1990, pp. 146-155.

Obermayer, James, "Eleven Simple Rules for Non-Cash Incentives," *Business Marketing,* Apr. 1984, pp. 44-48.

Paul, Ron, "Organizing for Marketing Planning," *Sales & Marketing Management* (Special Report), pp. 2-4.

"Plan or Perish," *Sales & Marketing Management,* May 18, 1981, pp. 45-46.

Powers, Thomas L., "Industrial Distribution Options: Trade-Offs to Consider," *Industrial Marketing Management,* vol. 18, Aug. 1989, pp. 155-161.

Pride, William M., and Ferrell, O.C., *Marketing: Concepts and Strategies,* 7th ed., Boston, MA: Houghton Mifflin Co., 1991.

Reeder, Robert R., Brierty, Edward G., and Reeder, Betty H., *Industrial Marketing, Analysis, Planning and Control,* Englewood Cliffs, NJ: Prentice-Hall, Inc., 1987.

Robinson, Mark, "Executive Support Systems," *Information Executive*, Fall 1990, pp. 34-36.

Ross, John Minor, "I Can't Get No (Computer) Satisfaction," *Information Executive*, Fall 1990, pp. 40-42.

Senn, James A., "Information System Strategies," *Business*, Oct.-Dec. 1989, pp. 43-47.

Shull, Joseph S., and Palmatier, George E., "Harnessing MRP II for Accurate Forecasts," *Business Marketing*, June 1985, pp. 90-96.

Spanner, Robert A., "How Much Trade Secret Security Is Enough?" *Business Marketing*, October 1984, pp. 70-88.

Survey of Current Business, published by the U.S. Department of Commerce/Bureau of Economic Analysis.

Sutton, Howard, *Competitive Intelligence* (Research Report No. 913), New York, NY: The Conference Board, 1988.

Sutton, Howard, *Rethinking the Company's Selling and Distribution Channels* (Report No. 885), New York, NY: The Conference Board, 1986.

Taylor, Thayer C., "Strategic Information Systems for Marketing," *Sales & Marketing Management*, July 1990, pp. 90-91.

Taylor, Thayer C., "How to Make a Better Fit Between Product and Customer," *Sales & Marketing Management*, August 1990, pp. 82-96.

"Ten Ways to Restore Vitality," *The Wall Street Journal*, Feb. 18, 1986, p. 31.

Urban, Glen L., Hauser, John R., and Dholakia, Nikhilesh, *Essentials of New Product Management*, Englewood Cliffs, NJ: Prentice-Hall, Inc. 1987.

Wagner, Jennifer L., "What Is End-Use Computing?" *Information Executive*, Fall 1990, pp. 24-26.

Wallis, Louis A., *Decision Support Systems for Marketing* (Research Report No. 923), New York, NY: The Conference Board, 1989.

Wallis, Louis A., "Marketing Priorities" (Research Bulletin 205), New York, NY: The Conference Board, 1987.

Wallis, Louis A., *Computers and the Sales Effort* (Report No. 884), New York, NY: The Conference Board, 1986.

Walsh, Dean, and Dahm, Joanne, "Going Flex—Four Adjustable Comp Plans That Work," *Sales & Marketing Management*, Sept. 1989, pp. 16-21.

Washburn, Stewart A., "How to Find the Manufacturers' Rep Who'll Really Work for You," *Business Marketing*, June 1983, pp. 82-86.

Index